T-PEOPLE

ISBN 978-1-4583-9257-2

Printed in USA by Lulu Publishing

Based On Actual Events

"As I write these recollections of women who survived, I hope my readers are taking careful note of why they did.

They screamed.
They fought.
They slammed doors in a stranger's face.
They ran.
They doubted glib stories.
They spotted flaws in those stories.
They were lucky enough to have someone step up and protect them."

— Ann Rule

En route through Framingham a shadowy extraterrestrial looms in the rear-view mirror. Traffic after the Norfolk Superior Court hearing session on Route 9 dies down to a standstill. Minutes earlier my client, a cardiac patient with congestive heart failure calls to re-hash the hearing on Defendants' *Motion to Dismiss*.. At a red-light the sun glints squarely in my right eye, seconds later the crashing of metal. ***SLAM!***

The car jolts forward several feet. Enough time to brace for impact. No one driving in front of me at the red light on Route 9. At least my seat belt was on. *Suburban Sprinkler* marks the sixteen-foot-long box truck that hit my car, totaling my modest light blue Honda Civic. Police offer to call an ambulance. Tell me to be grateful the truck did not push my car forward fifteen feet and off the road. No police report. My injuries not severe at first.

S.S. hits right about when the *Esler v. Sylvia-Reardon* FMLA case gets scheduled for a *Motion to Dismiss*. Out of work for a month to rehabilitate. S.S. claims to have fallen asleep at the wheel during rush hour.

In his 2019 book, *Catch and Kill: Lies, Spies, and a Conspiracy to Protect Predators* Ronan Farrow describes a ninja form of intimidation and retaliation leveled against women who came forward to accuse a powerful Hollywood player. In an interview about his book, Farrow describes, "A set of tools he truly did not know were available to the most powerful men when they are bent on stopping allegations against them." These tools include undercover agents who befriend accusers to obtain privileged information and then use it against the accuser should they decide to come forward. Farrow describes a byzantine network of front organizations, illegals, and trolls posing to collect personal information. Data brokers buying and selling information to the intelligence agencies.[1] The information culled may not even be dependable, but that does not matter in a world like theirs.

It is difficult to imagine a more devious way to silence an opponent. Such tools guarantee a powerful, wealthy opponent that their accuser and anyone with the guts to stand up to them will experience intimidation, dissipation of social capital and other resources, in the hope that nobody, but especially not their intended victim will have the presence of mind, the funds, or even the ability to identify the true source of the abuse, and therefore, unable to identify an attorney without a conflict of interest or a financial motive connected to the predator to ethically represent the interests of whistleblower.[2] There go your 7th Amendment rights, the right to a trial by jury.

The book documents experiences with predators. Their tactics are similar to those identified in Ronan Farrow's book *Catch and Kill*. More recently, the Center for Democracy and Technology published an article on the targeting of citizens by the use of 3rd party proxies who feed this information to intelligence operatives.[3] When a woman first notices signs of stalking, the predator has been stalking her for a long time.

In *The Gift of Fear* Gavin de Becker identifies patterns in stories of violence and abuse to highlight the inherent predictability of violence. *The Gift of Fear* identifies Forced Teaming, Charm and Niceness, Too Many Details, Typecasting, Loansharking, Unsolicited Promises, Discounting "No." These are the calling cards of a predator. This book identifies PINS (pre-incident identifiers) in encounters with abusers, often those who view whistleblower advocacy as worthy of containment, punishment, and intimidation. Recognize the predator's pattern, and its threat of violence becomes more predictable.

One helpful female surgeon tells me every operation has own signature style. If you look closely enough at the work, after a while the person who did it becomes easily recognizable. Even the type of training, the tools or treatments used, the preferred aesthetic and related preferences unique to the operator become easily recognizable. It takes time to get to that point, but once you recognize the work, each time it reappears it is like a authenticating a signature. This is not as an indictment necessarily but the reality.

This book attempts to recognize the predator's pattern and goes one step further. Women cannot afford not to recognize the underground alliance of predators because your life and livelihood may depend on it. In the media marketplace today, attention is the product. This attention can easily turn into grooming behavior, by now well-known tool of the predator. "Grooming is a form of abuse that involves manipulating someone until they're isolated, dependent, and more vulnerable to exploitation."[4] The quality of victims lives, their experience of connectedness, and the quality of their relationships looks quite different before the abuse started as compared with after the victim has begun to recognize the abuse and taken steps to protect him or herself. If this book can help you to identify the predators in your life, all the better.

Although this story is told through female eyes, this is not solely an issue for women. Men can just as easily be victimized by predators whether they are church leaders, politicians, or members of law enforcement or the judiciary -- anywhere power can be abused. These are predators getting special cover, often employed under government contracts delegated to non-state actors, and therefore, not accountable as they should be to *We the People*.

There are two set of rules. One for the predators, a more favorable set of rules, and a far more expensive set of rules for the victimized. While predators sell our Constitutional rights out from under us, basic requests for public accountability go unanswered. "Our state's public records law is in place to ensure an open, accessible, and accountable government, especially important when it comes to promoting public confidence in law enforcement," said Jillian Fennimore, a spokesperson for Healey, in a statement. "Following repeated failures by the Boston Police Department to produce these records, we are seeking an order from the court that they must be turned over."[5] Litigation attempts to hold predators in official positions accountable is necessary, however, *We the People* pay the attorney's fees, costs, and damages. This mischief encourages corruption, while lowering the quality of life and standard of living for everyone. This book recognizes the importance of making predators less invisible. This is my personal experience beyond the Courtrooms of Worcester County.

I.

A West German national calling himself Nils lurks on social media. A cardiologist by training, he works to complete a medical residency at the Brigham through a visa exchange program. Smokes Camels. Drinks whisky. Lives in Brookline, a short bike ride to work. A specialist in the drugs Coumadin and Warfarin, he describes rounds and the types of drug cases on which he consults. Warfarin, a chelation experts use to eradicate rats. The kind of guy who enjoys casual conversation about *The Framingham Study,* and Low-T over a large mushroom pizza while I seriously question my sense of smell. Aryan, 6 foot 2 inches tall, middle-aged, bald, arrogant, with partially waxed shoulders. Clone Gene Hackman, give him a delayed West German cousin, give him a medical license, and put him in high-waisted, tight designer jeans. Get the picture? Didn't have a car.

"BMW is the only car I drive." A Hohenschönhausen situation involving someone skilled in planting anti-personal landmines. Psychopaths study their victims to cultivate linguistic mirroring. It is a way to create a false sense of connection. A red flag. On the other hand, when psychopaths rely on bad information, and use this false information to create a connection, they become immediately identifiable as the predator they truly are. Every time a new predator introduces himself with the same recognizable pattern it is like recognizing the same person over and over again. They are all the same man with the same M.O. Apologies in advance to the reader when this gets repetitive. The result of entitled men stuck in a false narrative.

What prompted this strange man who works at the Brigham to contact me on social media? Nils describes a former fiancée as a borderliner.[1] The description he provides, more clinical than romantic, suggests a view of women as hopeless cases – damaged goods.[6] As this stranger continues speaking, elaborating on his fascination with the Framingham Study and Low-T, he observes any micro-reaction, evaluating, measuring, wearing a smiling mask,…waiting to pounce. He says his father

---

[1] *Typecasting*

instructs him to dump the fiancée after a ten-year courtship.

The *damaged goods theory*, the premise for second class treatment and euthanasia of the mentally ill under the Nazi *T4 Aktion*, provides the same premise for misogynistic treatment of his girlfriend as disposable. Revisionist history features prominently in conversations with holocaust deniers, predators, and those seeking to use the misery of others as a jumping off point to start a conversation.

The documentary *Assholes, a Theory* features a former female Canadian RCMP named Waterloo who reports gender-based harassment in her department. The story casts Waterloo as a cautionary tale. The film's narrative urges its viewer to file the Waterloo case under "things to avoid or else that's what you get." The case led to further upheaval when two internal inspectors were similarly ousted over allegations its "internal affairs division made up evidence to silence whistleblower cops."[7] The documentary's premise, one most people can agree on, that assholery in the workplace should be avoided, noticeably omits the eugenics movement's role in the rise of the Nazis. Re-writing history puts the system of justice at risk of repeating the same patterns of abuse. My strange German confrère continues,

"He is just looking out for my best interests." *T4 Aktion,* considered a precursor to the Holocaust, advances the rationale that euthanasia saves the state money.

"My father was a high-ranking Nazi during WWII." He smiles, again, watching and waiting for my expression. The Nazi party, officially, the National Socialist German Workers' Party arose to power after WWI under a populist paramilitary *Freikorps.* Freikorps means volunteer in German. Freikorps expanded membership through the Nazi propaganda machine, aimed at youth organizations, most notably, Hitler Youth[8] to indoctrinate members while they were young. Nils continues,

"Yes, but everyone was pro-Nazi at that time in Europe. 99% of Europe at the time was pro-Hitler and pro-Nazi. My father did very well during the war." After Kristallnacht, the Nazis sanitized official propaganda, replacing it with rallies, films, and books intended to promote escapism from the brutality of the Nazi war machine. They understood that blasting their ideology would not work. To convert potential followers, they needed a constant flow of entertainment casting the Nazis as knights in shining armor.

"Does your father have a change of opinion now, or does he still have the views of the former Nazi party?"

"Nobody talks about WWII. It causes too much distress." Dinner with Nazi Nils resembles more of a Hohenschönhausen situation, the institution feared for psychological torture. Who wants an invitation to dine with someone related to an institution whose leadership actively bets against its' constituents in a covert game of information warfare?[9] "This is how a society destroys itself," one German activist targeted by Stasi states.[10] "It is the height of naivete to think that once collected this information won't be used."

Interracial marriage was not legal under the Nazis, where the *Law for the Prevention of Hereditarily Diseased Offspring* requires documentation of mixed or half-breed offspring.[11] Vestiges of Rassenhygiene[12] remain alive today, although throughout the 1950s and 1960s physicians regularly enforced it at renowned hospitals in the United States long after the Nazis were defeated due to the popularity of eugenics. It did not require being German or even affiliated with the Nazi party, because its genesis was the eugenics ideology that promoted the idea of a pure master race.

Mercy killings under the Nazis were carried out by personal physicians.[13] Doctors asked questions and quietly marked patients medical record with a cross. The cross indicated the patient should be euthanized. Hitler's personal physicians politicized this idea. Under the government decree, actual examination was unnecessary, "It is sufficient to extract from the files the reasons for their arrest (often very extensive!) and to record them on the questionnaires."[14] Dr. Karl Brandt and Chancellery chief Philipp Bouhler were "charged with responsibility for expanding the authority of physicians...so that patients considered incurable, according to the best available human judgment of their state of health, can be granted a mercy killing."[15] This was known as the T4 program, a program about gassing people to death based upon a vicious and politicized dossier of lies. "This is the nature of secret government organizations. The only way to protect the people's privacy is not to allow the government to collect their information in the first place."...

According to Robert Lifton, when the Second World War began in September 1939, T4 began to employ less rigorous standards of assessment, a quicker approval process, casting a wider net successfully ensnaring older children and adolescents in the T4 euthanasia program. After doctors identified their victims, T4 became operational. T4 Operation took place from September 1939 until the end of the war in 1945 killing between 275,000 to 300,000 people in psychiatric hospitals, someone of them run by religious institutions. This net includes various borderline or limited impairments in children of different ages, culminating in the killing of those designated as juvenile delinquents. Jewish children could be placed in the net primarily because they were Jewish; and at one of the institutions, a special department was set up for 'minor Jewish-Aryan half-breeds.[16]

A female physician involved in cancer research in San Francisco advises me cancer growth relates to being immunocompromised. In her opinion, life with an abuser exposes an individual to unusually high levels of unremitting stress, creating the ideal environment for tumor or cancer growth. She was attempting to explain how a healthy 28-year-old woman wound up with cancer, and its connection to a sabotaging, toxic man, including a former male physician she opined committed malpractice. Although anecdotal, removing the abuser lead to immediate health improvement. This is a theory with data to support it, especially considering the number one cause of death in abused women is leaving their abusers. A history of abuse tends to attract abusers; it is almost like they can smell vulnerability on former victims. Improving the quality of training and exposing significant abuses serves the public. Police misconduct litigation often does little to change the rate of civil rights abuse because there is no personal accountability.[17] The downside for taxpayers is that the current system indemnifies officers even if their conduct violates the Constitution. Even though civil rights lawsuits are paid by *We the People*, officials have worked on the public dime to prevent the public from knowing about the existence of such lawsuits, and how much money has been spent.[18] At the same time, their victims are left unrepresented. Civil rights cases are winnable, and they do provide for attorney's fees after resolution of a prevailing case– but the time to get to a jury is often four to five years. That is a long time to wait and only very few attorneys wait that long while representing clients, running an office, and tending to all the other necessities of life.

"You want go Dutch?" This man's father carries out the orders of the Third Reich. *No.* He should pay his own way. *We the People* should support individual liability for officers caught violating the Constitutional rights of U.S. Citizens.[19]

"Sometimes you have to push the envelope." For a physician to say all of this to a woman he targets on social media signals predation by a stranger with power in the medical-defense complex. This is the nature of a psychopath -- they tend to repeat patterns.

DAEDALUS CONSTRUCTS WINGS FOR HIS SON ICARUS[20]

II.

Daedalus contacts me on social media, or an individual going by that name. Daedalus, the creator of the Labyrinth mysteriously crosses my path in my second year of law school. It was fall, approaching mid-terms. A Cambridge native, he lives close to Harvard University within walking distance from my tiny Trowbridge Street apartment. Daedalus' wife has cancer. She is dying; he seeks company, not a romantic companion. He has been married to his wife for almost 50 years. He is a Jew; a learned man in an advisory role to hierarchy of the Catholic Diocese,[21] private airlines, and conservative educational institutions including a law school. He is also a professor at Boston College, a predominantly white Catholic School on the outskirts of Boston.

Daedalus is first mentioned in roughly 1400 BC n the Knossian Linear B tablets. He is later mentioned by Homer as the creator of the Shield of Achilles. The architect for the Labyrinth, an elaborate, confusing structure designed and built by the legendary artificer for King Minos of Crete at Knossos. Contemporary scholars and enthusiasts observe a distinction between the *labyrinth* and the *maze*. A unicursal *labyrinth* has only a single path to the center. Daedalus creates a labyrinth in this sense has an unambiguous route to the center and back and presents no navigational challenge. No way out exists without the permission of the architect.

The *labyrinth's* function was to hold the Minotaur, the monster. In the modern labyrinth, the Minotaur, like a demon, populates spaces where it can silently wreak the most havoc. Locking someone inside the labyrinth with the Minotaur guarantees a slow and painful death. An agonizing death, much like the experience women had with Picasso, "After he had spent many nights extracting their essence, once they were bled dry, he would dispose of them."[22] It creeps into spaces, disintegrating the unwary, measure by measure.

Daedalus warns Icarus first of complacency and then of hubris, instructing him to fly neither too low nor too high, lest the sea's dampness clog his wings or the sun's heat melt them. Icarus and Daedalus attempt to escape from Crete by means of wings that Daedalus constructs from feathers and wax. The myth gave rise to the idiom "don't fly too close to the sun." My computer seizes and spontaneously combusts [23] during an arbitration class that year,

"There is no smoking in the classroom."

Daedalus, the architect for this Labyrinth protects a byzantine network of allied enforcers. In order to be sent to the Labyrinth,[24] an elaborate for-profit prison that serves an agenda with no opposition in this echo chamber, an offering to the bull needed to be made. *Maze* refers to a complex branching multicausal puzzle with choices. Those lucky enough to reside in the *maze* instead of suffering banishment to the labyrinth get preferential treatment. They have choices. Free will.

We control the horizontal...

Daedalus had so cunningly made the Labyrinth that he could barely escape it after he built it. This is the double-edge axe Daedalus wields in this upside-down world. Icarus ignores Daedalus' instructions not to fly too close to the sun, causing the **wax** in his wings to melt. He tumbles out of the sky, falls into the sea, and drowns. We would meet again under surprising circumstances, reconnected by Ursa Major and Ursa Minor, aligning the Orsini clan in the sky.

'We now approach the city known as Dis[25]...

III.

Long before we reach the bottom of that lofty Tower, our eyes travel upwards to its lofty summit... An irresistible attic rental space on CL appears out of the blue for $625.[26] Trowbridge Street, a building where the slamming front door practically fell off its hinges transforms a $1300 studio magically to an airy three flight walkup in the pitched attic of an expensively renovated 1880s Somerville home at 72 Boston Street. Three times the size, and less than half the price, on a quiet one-way street means walking to the bus, a city bus with a large woman wearing SpongeBob cartoon regalia every single day. A murder across the street suggests violent crime in the neighborhood, although this appears to be an aberration. The new place, a short drive from the Winter Hill neighborhood of Whitey Bulger fame.

The landlord belongs to what she describes as a support group for women, disclosing her work as a leader in her group. As a trainer for other women, she advises others seeking to learn how to "be a strong woman." Tells me, in regard to my goal of graduating from law school and working as an attorney, "You will compete with men too much…You'll never make it." Seems invested in the assumption that my legal career will end in folly. Among the available barometers for measuring female actualization, one of the more distorted versions to suddenly wander across my path. This ideology, that competition with men is bad for you, means rationalizing all kinds of covert sabotage of other women. The cult known as Sterling Relationship Institute, a group run by A. Jason Sterling, espouses the idea,

"Women have become too much like men[2], Men have become too much like women, and therefore, the sexes must work to keep the sexes polarized, to achieve happier male-to-female relationships." She openly acknowledges this is a cult built on a one-sided foundation. In any event, this ideology will make her outwardly successful because *she will be married*. Advice on women's actualization from a for-profit cult really would not concern me, except for the fact that it took on the force of law in this home with no doors.

The man is expected to be a good provider, and the woman is expected to be grateful and dutiful. She tells me, "All men are assholes" and that it is up to a woman to "be strong enough" to withstand all of his assholery. Weak women do not understand this

_____

[2] *Typecasting.*

simple concept, seemingly a vestige of 1950s stay at home and be a housewife culture, and that is why they cannot find happiness. A woman must "Leave a man better than she found him." To me this sounds like gibberish.

To be an alpha in this culture requires buying in to the twisted theory. The Sterling courses, fifteen years ago, cost the participants anywhere from $4,400 to well over $8000 for educational seminars. Leaders are encouraged to front the cost in exchange for working it off, a form of debt slavery. In addition to that awkward financial arrangement, the seminars record intimacies shared on film. Due to some exceedingly broad waivers, this sounds eerily like Jim Jones to me. Pass the Kool-Aid.

The Sterling theory posits polarization of the sexes increases sexual tension, empowering women to navigate the *Cycle of Abuse*, a term popularized by Lenore Walker in 1979, by using their sexual "feminine essence." "You are a woman with a man inside watching a woman. You are your own voyeur."[27] A not-so-subtle form of sexual bartering at the heart of this theory, women perform sexual kindnesses in exchange for male protection, and women show their gratitude by foisting this agenda on unprotected females, reinforcing a dysfunctional and abusive power center. Like a form of communal life where the women police each other for the illusion of safety. The person most likely to benefit from the Sterling model is the for-profit prison guard, A. Jason Sterling. Postings online suggest that the group may be based on EST, a group for divorcing couples popularized in the 1970s featured in *The Americans*.

Downstairs, neighbors get invited to attend classes to be worked off over time. Amway, probably the most recognizable type of Ponzi scam seeks new recruits to drum false hope into their psyche, then teaches followers to robotically repeat this message like a nervous tick. One of the selling points for joining the group is to help guide others who, "Have suffered intense rejection." Rejecting the dominant culture cannot be cured by joining a cult that rewards oppression.

At the time, I am in law school, working full time and in my spare time running half marathons. Not exactly susceptible to groupthink. After numerous conversations about my lack of interest, she introduces me to a man. The introduction goes like this,

"This is a man who is not to be trusted," This is her special friend, a man who barters his reward in places where eyes are not looking. After introducing me to this man *not to be trusted*, she offers me Percocet without a prescription. Like the airy affordable attic apartment, it is bait. In the mind of this for-profit cult trainer and top photographer, insinuating her friend, a DEA agent to sabotage her tenant is fair game. At the same time, she shows me her bookshelf and tells me to "Borrow any book I want."

In her collection, Nancy *Friday*. One of the stories depicts a woman fornicating with an 800-pound gorilla. An unusual book for any woman to have on her bookshelf, but in particular a woman who works in a cult that promotes the idea of female second class citizens. If anyone has an 800-pound gorilla in their psyche it would have to be someone promoting the idea of women as second-class citizens. It is the kind of book that someone probably plants in her bookshelf to set off landmines later. From where did she learn how to plant anti-personal landmines like this? From s*omeone not to be trusted*. In evaluating people, she often refers to "how they look on paper" versus what they are like in person. People who evaluate other people *on paper* tend to be bureaucrats creating dossiers, often fabricated from whole cloth. They also tend to like planting things that prove they were right all along. Thought police. A red flag.

What provokes this preemptive defense involving drugs, apartments with no doors, and planted books involving aberrant fantasies, and evaluating people *on paper*? My vocal criticism of her for profit cult. To be targeted, agents have to provide a reason, even a false one involving typecasting. An insidious attack presumably will never be reported to the authorities. *They are the authorities.* In the Labyrinth a DEA agent mirrors Daedalus in a covert game of treachery while they cover each other's tracks. *The Art of Self Defense* comes to mind.

In quiet stairwells, the downstairs neighbors commiserate about our mind-controlled landlord while their cat wanders up three flights of stairs to sit on the floor in the attic. Inside the triangular ceilinged bedroom, a small window opens at night slightly at the front and another at the back. The chill of the late fall air creeps inside. Inside my dreams a man, a dark-haired man sees everything, like someone remotely viewing my every thought. A most vivid dream, in technicolor, the kind that makes you wonder what decade it is upon awakening. My waking eyes see the room looks the same, the sun through the windows catches the dust floats on a bias mid-air. Is it the 1950s? No, it might as well be the late 1800s. How strange to live with eyes upon every deed, inside our dreams, awakening us to griffins perched atop our chests in the middle of the night.

KNIGHT of CUPS.

IV.

On a crisp winter night, after foliage season, tree branches reach over city streets like gothic spires. At Dali, the Spanish restaurant where Nils met me in Somerville, over hot stone grilled beef, nerdy conversation on the subject of military grade weapons, nanotechnology and cyberwarfare ensues. A former Bain & Company consultant, he provides services to leaders. Bain has over the years been labeled the "KGB of Consulting," or a "Moonie commune" run by the "Reverend" Bain."[28] An entrepreneur and a principal in a nanotechnology firm and a graduate of Harvard Business School (HBS) the man is a mystery wrapped in an enigma.

Outside the restaurant we get into a beige Toyota Highlander and cross the Charles, continuing through Newton. Pulling up a long wide driveway to an enormous Waban home to a three-car garage. In one bay his prized antique red jaguar. Over the threshold inside the home, a purchase from a couple going through a terrible divorce.

In the middle of his living room sits an intricately carved oak throne, rust-colored upholstery, and medieval claw feet. On the walls, ancient tapestries depicting unicorns.[29] Expensive framed portraits of King Arthur, Guinevere, and the Knights of the Round Table feature prominently in the overall theme. Medieval meets high-tech vampire. The wife loves indoor plants. At the end of a long hallway painted lavender, a rounded wall of vines from ceiling to the floor. Strangely, of all the same variety.

Previous owners fought a lot and slammed the doors so often that he had to replace the door. A collector of dragons, describing a private room, a repository for the dragons he collects. Describing thousands of them, like trophies stacked up high on a table, of all different colors, shapes, and sizes. G.S.'s back yard contains a large thirteen-foot bronze dragon imported from China. Chasing the dragon, a term synonymous with brown heroin, the kind of drug that brings in cash. He says he hopes to deck each room out in its own elaborate theme. The neighbor has a Zen Garden he spent over $200,000 installing. [3] Tells me he checked it out once. Something about a lush green Tea Garden and a helicopter pad with a Japanese bridge. He describes a self-melting driveway with a substrata electric grid powerful enough to make snow and ice melt with the flock of a switch from his front door. He has not put it in yet. The underground electricity makes snow evaporate into thin air. A charming man, his favorite television series was *Alias,* the action thriller created by J.J. Abrams.

 *e are controlling transmission...*

---

[3] An exceedingly precise number. Rounding off money.

In the rented attic in Somerville, G. reveals to me an experience observing lasers or directed-energy weapons. G tells me about laser beam-type weapons and their capabilities. A big fan of artificial intelligence, cryptically, "What are you going to do, quote music lyrics in your legal arguments?"

"Yes, why not?" Think of numbers in music like gap-fillers. Music is like math. If you Every musical note has a corresponding frequency. Middle C for example vibrates at 261 hertz. Which means that any piece of music can be expressed as an equation. …Encoded within the tune a fuel source. The military applications alone would be unlimited.[30] A behavior modification tool suitable for a designated shrew, a draconian one with no way to legally cite it. The trick, to manipulate decision-making by remotely tugging on the reigns.[31]

Since 1997, Bandler has claimed, "Neuro Linguistic Programming (NLP) is based on finding out what works and formalizing it. In order to formalize patterns, I utilized everything from linguistics to holography…The models that constitute NLP are all formal models based on mathematical, logical principles such as predicate calculus and the mathematical equations underlying holography." The tool has its limitations.

During one mind-control experiment a directed energy beam prompts speech. He describes a third party prompting an individual to mimic scripted conversation word-for-word. The mechanism was a laser beam combined with a computer involving the use of RF-technology. He suggests the Electronic Communications Protection Act (ECPA) may be an issue. A mind-control device with Satanic overtones.

"You've got potential."[32] Flatterer.

He describes seeing an individual sitting in front of or near a computer; an electronic current directed at the person, running through them prompting them to speak not just a word or two, but extensive dialogue. Words directed by a third-party. Compelled speech. Once married, however, the marriage annulled after one day. Says the woman changed her mind. There is something cold, so cold about this man. He is a Caucasian, middle aged, clean-cut, highly intelligent male, talking about mind control techniques, unquestionably unconstitutional, and cyberwarfare. His face a reptilian mask, into the idea of meshing medieval and transhumanist ideas. Speaking without words, a foreshadowing of violence.

"It was a mistake," he says unapologetically. Compelled speech is no mistake. To hear this highly intelligent Hungarian speak so casually about marriage, annulment, and laser beam weapons in the same conversation makes me uneasy. It was unsettling. Later he calls to tell me of a new hire for his business. Found someone gifted in the marketing arts. Three gym memberships as well, though he says he rarely sees any of them.

"I've never done this before. But I prefer someone who writes romance novels." Says he met the romance novelist, at the Four Seasons Hotel. Tells me about his meetings with investors, and his search for VC money. Approaching investors, he seeks venture capital. For what, *She Was a Teenage Mind Control Slave?*

"We'll have to visit you out there in Westborough." *This man knows where I live.* The Waban home registers to a Gabriel. Angels can be vicious creatures. A YouTube search reveals a proponent of eugenics.[33] The types of weapons the organization develops are the kinds of weapons the Nazis used against marginalized members of society…is he an *Angel of Death?* Who is really the pawn in a deal for mind-control technology? All roads in the Labyrinth lead back to this charming man….*Alias.*

V.

Driving away from The Chophouse the radio plays *I'm On Fire.* The sky a dark velvet blue. The bars and storefronts dark, sidewalks empty, no one around at all. Two blocks past Macs Diner, after an evening out with a known police informant whose boyfriend owns a funeral parlor with a crematorium in the basement, an antique beige sedan follows too closely. All of a sudden, *a* loud thrashing of metal, and stillness. The streets were dry and cold. There didn't seem to be anyone else on the road. No one to witness. This was the third time. Six months ago, a commercial box window washing truck crashes into the car en route home from the Superior Court parked in bumper-to-bumper traffic. Ten weeks later, a stranger hits while pulling out of the physical therapy provider's parking lot. Barely out of the doctor's office when the lurking malfeasant smashes the bumper. The first accident totals the civic and tonight's accident both happened on Route 9. A quick look in my rear-view mirror before the man stares in from outside the window.

"Don't call the cops." The man stood outside looking in. Sitting in the dark with this stranger feels like a good time to lock the door. In that light, he looked like Ted Bundy, clean cut, professional working man, Caucasian with an average height and build, somewhat nervous. Who knew what was going on inside the mind of a complete stranger? He could easily have a machete inside his jacket. He was probably intoxicated.

"I was just at the Chophouse." Maybe he was a really experienced serial killer, the invisible kind that sneaks up and first appears to be perfectly normal, pretending to be normal so that he could do something terribly romantic, *Black Dahlia romantic.*

Hunting in the dark for something to sink its teeth into, leaving his signature sparged peanuts sprinkled all over my corpse. All during this interlude on the side of a dark street off Route 9 alone and in need of help.

"I didn't see you at the Chophouse. Did you see me?" not sure the answer would make this situation any less creepy. Something about him reminds me of a glass of *Tresor.* "I will give you $10000.00 right now. Please just don't call the cops."

He opens his checkbook and starts writing. That was a first. Serial killers generally do not write out arbitrarily large checks. Why $10,000? Not wanting to end up starring as a murder victim on *Unsolved Mysteries.* Should the amount of money make me feel less guarded, or more concerned? Closing the driver side window, gesturing to need a minute. Still at the window, the man said in a voice loud enough to hear inside the car,

"I am going through a divorce right now and my wife will crucify me if this gets back to her." This sounds scripted. What possible relevance would a minor car accident have in a divorce? A check for $10,000 would likely be discoverable in a divorce, even if the check was written on a business account, because it would be considered community property, assuming the marriage is legitimate and not based on fraud. Problematic in this exchange, the fact that my depositing of a third party's $10,000 check would make my personal checking account discoverable to this stranger, who could be a serial killer. This seems more like a predator out hunting for food. The comment makes me decide to call an attorney who helped me before. Luckily, he answers though it was already 10:30 on a school night.

"Hey, what's up?"

"Sorry to bother you this late at night."

"It's ok..."

"I have a situation."

"What's up?"

"Some guy just hit my car, nothing major, but he is offering to write me a check for $10000 which seems kind of weird..."

"Where are you."

"Side of a road."

"Get yourself to a parking lot where you are under some lights, hopefully one with more people around," he suggests. Under the lights in a local bank parking lot, a camera would pick up on anything the stranger might pull to make what at first seemed to be an accident, turn into something less accidental.

"Put him on the phone." Putting the strange man on the phone with the attorney gave me a minute. Getting back on the phone with him after about ten minutes. They both wonder whether the guy followed from the Chophouse. Didn't see anything before he hit. The whole thing seemed so bizarre. The attorney says the guy said he was afraid that a legal claim would affect his custody rights in his pending divorce. *What custody rights?*

"Get out of there. Make sure he doesn't follow you. If he does try to follow you home call me back." After taking a minute to collect my nerves, watching, waiting, and hoping the strange man would drive away first, he didn't. Not sure whether the guy was intoxicated or if the whole thing was staged. Could he be a cop, maybe working off-duty and wanting to avoid trouble himself? Either way this night needs no more problems. Driving away towards home a different way. For the past twenty years, no accidents. Now three within six months all of them re-injuring my back and creating more red tape. At home, the walls stare back at me until sleep casts its spell.

In the early afternoon, the crashing of metal and a loud T H U D causes the walls of the apartment to shake me awake. Off the and up over the curb, into a bush, a stranger's sedan finally lands in the front yard quietly rattling. The final landing spot in the garden was about six feet past the sidewalk. A raucous worse than the damage. The intrusion pulls a tall red bush up from its roots. Thankfully, no one was hurt. The commotion drew the attention of several police cars, the fire department and neighbors walking by.

Such a confounding encounter on Shrewsbury Street the night before, leads me to an online search. Improbably, the driver's last name was also the last name of a client. His first name, John could easily be a cover. What could be more common than John? The last name was Esler was uncommon. It was the first time I had ever heard the name *Esler* besides having a client by that name. Could it be a coincidence? The client's name was public record. Client denies being any relation. She thought it was odd. Three accidents in less than six months? Search results display the name John Esler as the owner of a flooring company. Flooring rhymes with boring. John Esler's Google results display a contentious flooring lawsuit.[34] The story could be fake, a story written by a fake entity storing vats of muriatic acid to rent out to their serial killer friends for dipping anyone who became a little too troublesome. It could all be a hoax. A search displays nothing about the divorce he blames for his odd behavior and a $10000 check. But that did not seem surprising at the time. The number 10000 was probably pulled out of thin air. A cover with no way to connect it. *Or was there?*

The second accident, just six weeks before involves, once again, a car hitting the rear bumper, this time pulling out of the parking lot of a doctor's office. By then I had a new vehicle. No less than a month after the purchase, a nondescript older vehicle in need of a car wash hits my car from behind. Travelling less than 25 miles per hour following me after PT. Dr. Miller cheerily writes me a prescription for SOMA because "It's less addictive."

SOMA, the drug from the utopian society in Aldous Huxley's book *Brave New World*, a society that follows three strict rules: no privacy, no family, no monogamy. Though there are superiors to lead the community, the entire system is governed by an unseen force called Intra.[35]

VI.

"Chief says someone out front has a mental health issue." The printout from LifeLock contains the address and name of a former officer who performs special favors for a Worcester Chief. Someone at the address accesses or tried to access my credit file. The property listed recently sold.

"I am just here to file a police report."

"We don't think that is identity theft. You stopped it."

"LifeLock recommends filing a police report."

"We won't do that." [36]

"Okay, why can't I just file a report to create a record?"

"We don't think that meets the requirements. [37] You could try going to the District Court, asking for victim services, and requesting a restraining order against the person who you think did it."

The first thing a Court will want to know is whether the victim reports the events to the police. Without a paper trail, the Court will be in a less tenable position, because how can a court act when there is no paper trail. Courts need official records. Maybe that is the point.

"A restraining order requires three separate events."

"Do you have three separate events?" While this police officer is asking me whether I have three separate events, another police officer is breaking into compartments inside my car. This presents another example of the covert warfare by local police betting against constituents.[38] It actually a good way to guarantee further abuse.

"Probably. But I am not going to waste my time trying to get a restraining order against this person." (See obstructionist tactics on previous page.)

"Why not? It is how you can hold them responsible for their actions. It is up to YOU to do that." As a trained police officer, especially one trained in mental health, this officer understands that the first thing victims get asked when they go to Court is whether they filed a police report. Why push a citizen to institute legal process in the District Court while ensuring that they will not have evidence of filing a police report? One reason might be to put the victim in the position of applying for a restraining order, having the request denied for not filing a people report, and raising questions about the victim's judgment for failing to report the incident to police. At a minimum, it serves to raise questions about a victim's credibility. This serves the abusers agenda by promoting an endless cycle of abuse. It does not serve victims.

Returning to my car, the glove and gun compartments sit wide open. Obnoxiously wide open like the splaying of a female sexual orifice. This occurrence at a place that holds itself out to the public as "We guarantee dignity and respect to every individual."[39]Advocates for domestic abuse protections often raise concerns about women fear reporting their abusers. This is an excellent example of reinforced dysfunction. This type of dysfunction can cost women their lives.

As I document notes related to illegal activity occurring at my residence -- vandalism of both of my cars, illegal entry into my residence, leaving seven propane gas tanks in my garage, and ordering and not receiving a motion sensor video camera to install in my car for protection – all while the local police refuse to accept a report – instead, blaming the victim.. Anyone think the local Chief has formed a preliminary opinion perhaps one that plays a role in this tidal wave of misconduct?[40]. P.O. Inspector General confirms by GPS that the video camera designed to record tampering with vehicles and police stops arrives at the P.O., somehow, disappears into thin air. Guess what's for dinner. Months later, notes written on the printout from LifeLock regarding the events, along with some related communications saved as a .pdf gets remotely scrubbed. Notes disappear into thin air. This is known as a wipe-out. Like the song of the same name by the Beach Boys.

It rubs the lotion
on its skin or else it gets
the hose again.

-Jame Gumb (Buffalo Bill)

VII.

Mulligan Sullivan, a defense attorney, and my opponent in the *Esler* case, wrote a letter to the bar requesting investigation into whether I have a disability. Sullivan's letter to the state bar occurs the year that the Supreme Judicial Court reinstates a verdict in favor of a nurse, a verdict his firm nullified, prolonging resolution of a matter filed in 2008 until well after 2017. The *get bent* message, originating from a defense attorney for the hospital obstructs our system of justice.[4] In 2018, a Suffolk County jury

---

[4] *See*, **Title II-3.5300 Unnecessary inquiries**. A public entity may not make unnecessary inquiries into the existence of a disability.

sides with plaintiffs in a retaliation case, awarding 28M, the highest plaintiffs verdict of that nature in history against the Brigham. *Gessy Toussaint et al. v. Brigham and Women's Hospital et al.*, 2014 WL 3639029, No. SUCV2014-2253 (Mass. Sup. Ct., filed 6/15/2014) "The timeline was the strongest piece of evidence.."[41]

Certainly, there is an intimidating message that livelihood is at risk when an opponent refers a prevailing colleague to be investigated for a nonexistent disability, particularly when that opponent represents the state's largest medical hierarchy. Contacting my former law school advisor, Andrew Perlman seeking Counsel, he refers me to Coach. They work on an ABA committee together. Coach suggests hiring an expensive expert for $350 to 450 dollars per hour in an attempt to prove that I am not disabled, by giving the defendants a window into my mental history through the eyes of a hired gun. A hired medical gun. When this is rejected, and a letter from the state's Disability Evaluation Services is offered to Rosenfeld, a letter substantiating no disability after direct examination by two medical providers. Rosenfeld withdraws, referring to a DOJ report and an MCAD complaint as "overly litigious."

It is a very strange feeling to repose trust in someone, rely on them to advance your career while also sensing that they are in fact viewing you as lunch based on stereotypes. It is a strange world indeed where the value in defending violent criminals outweighs the importance of fighting misogyny and gender discrimination. The legal profession has a significant problem with gender bias, and they are in complete denial about it. They would rather cover up gender bias, so that privileged elite men can exercise their right to disparage women in coded jargon, then deny the blatant misogyny inherent in this duplicitousness. At a BBO hearing, *my attorney* turns to me and says,

"Now that is someone I would want to be my daughter."[42] She was in her 20's petite and blond. I am not a size 14 or interested in playing the role of anyone's daughter and doubt the receptionist or anyone at the BBO would have found this objectification charming. For the crime of objecting to being cut down to size, reporting it to the DOJ, and filing an MCAD complaint against an underground union enforcer, the Indulgence cost $200,000+. The message – asserting gender other perceived bias will not be good for business.

"In today's world, the power to absolve debt is greater than the power of forgiveness." A Papal Indulgence is the remission by the Church, on specified conditions, of the whole or a part of the debt of satisfaction remaining due for sin.[43] Papal Indulgences, as a practice were outlawed 500 years ago by Martin Luther in 1517.[44] Simony originates from the Biblical passages Acts 8:9,13,18–24. For $200,000 a permanent abuse prevention order preventing the unremitting attacks on privacy should have been a fair enough exchange. It is more like a Japanese bridge flowing to a next-door neighbor's Zen Garden.

*W*e control the vertical...

Right about then, the newly christened Mass General Brigham begins to liaise with Westborough Town management to plan to open a facility nearby.[45] Mass General Brigham meets with the Town "to expand the total number of patients and generate new business."[46] The hospital pays no taxes. Instead, Mass General Brigham pays the Town directly into their general fund, which is the first agreement of its kind.[47] Generally speaking, this is also the fund from which the police budget gets appropriated. [*See FN 39*]

More recently, after an independent civil investigation, AG Martha Healey has criticized Mass General Brigham's expansion into the suburbs.[48] Healey's investigation concludes that expansion of the state's largest health care system will ultimately increase health care spending statewide, while netting the health system an estimated $385 million a year in profits, according to a report released Wednesday by Attorney General Maura Healey, raising questions about the expansion's impacts on overall health care costs in the state.[49]

Juries have held both Mass General and the Brigham responsible for retaliation in several high-profile cases. "[It's] sending a message to the Brigham and other institutions that retaliating against someone for standing up for what's right won't be tolerated."[50] According to an attorney who tried the case, the Brigham engaged in a pattern of retaliation against witnesses and their family members in spaces outside the hospital -- private places outside the control of the employer. Retaliation often includes punishment through means that are difficult if not possible for the target to document. The Brigham "strongly disagreed."

During the initial phases of the Mass General Brigham expansion, a client hears beeping noises during privileged conversations. Opposing counsel suggests reporting this abuse to the police. That will go well. Another interesting exercise in futility.

An audible tap or interference with communications is because "Someone wants to intimidate you or your sources."[51] Electronic tweaking, chirping, and hissing pervades the atmosphere like Styrofoam peanuts packed into a box a little too tightly. In addition to slut-shaming, they now have dystopian mental health gaslighting. A post-war re-education camp for women. *Down Girl.*

Those who cannot remember the past are condemned to repeat it.[52]

VIII.

Sometime in 2018, a man with a variation on a Dutch-sounding *Vans* family name contacts me seeking representation. Robert Evans (R.E.) claims that his company needs to hire me in a David versus Goliath type matter. R tells me that he hears about my good reputation from an individual he does not name. R claims predecessor counsel, a Columbia Law grad, overcharges him. Acknowledges that she got the case through the most difficult stages of litigation, through summary judgment, and that his firing her after that point was "unheard of." In addition, he states that the work performed by the competitor was deemed acceptable, but, according to R., his former female attorney covers up malpractice.[5] All of that sounds exceedingly specific.

Of course, these two things do not really fit together. If the work was deemed acceptable, there was nothing wrong. He says he would never go after her for any malpractice. Probably because there was no malpractice to go after, or the gymnastics feigned to make her appear blameworthy, an accident, actually presents a phony case of sandbagging. Then again, if the entire matter was a sham, bringing a sham malpractice case to short a sum of money against this poor woman would be tantamount to fraud. What is Mr. Van's up to?

W e control the image

make it flutter.

---

[5] **Too many details.** If a person is lying they will add excessive details to make themselves sound more credible to their chosen victim. De Becker, The Gift of Fear (1997).

I wanted to better understand *R's* tankless water heater operation. The female principal, Melissa, does not appear at the initial consultation. **Melissa needs independent counsel.** Melissa might be a pawn; she entered a business-type marriage under false pretenses. She might be bound by an agent, an agent who usurps her voice in financial matters directly affecting her earning power, and, to make matters worse, she is without knowledge of the ways her rights are being abused. When she finds out, to whom will she report the abuse, her reptilian husband? A silent partnership with a reptile that abuses her rights, insults her intelligence, and discards her like garbage. Report it to the authorities? *These reptiles are the authorities.*

Flings at the Secretary of State division of corporations inform me that R and his wife now live in Sutton, a wealthy suburb West of Boston. A manufacturer incorporated in 2006 with a registered office located at 45 McGregory Road, Sturbridge, Massachusetts.

"Where would your office headquarters be? Can I check it out?"

"It's a rats nest. You don't want to go there," he smiles. You must be one of the rats. As Atwood correctly points out, "A rat in a maze is free to go anywhere, as long as it stays inside the maze." The reptiles live in a maze; a woman must survive the labyrinth.

"What is the address?"

"It's off main street, near the Worcester Courthouse." The front company's script leaves the wife out of any discussions or decision-making. Cryptically he asks, "What ever happened to General Electric?"

"GE?" The timing of R.E.'s appearance, following on the heels of the *Esler* litigation, might suggest an ulterior motive. Does it have anything to do with a *terrible divorce?*

"If we win, I want to give you 3% of the gross[6] in addition to your regular hourly rate." In a commercial paper case.

---

[6] **The Unsolicited Promise**. A promise to do (or not do) something when no such promise is asked for; **this usually means that such a promise will be broken**. For example: an unsolicited, "I promise I'll leave you alone after this," usually means the chosen victim will not be left alone. Similarly, an unsolicited "I promise I won't hurt you" usually means the person intends to hurt their chosen victim, de Becker, The Gift of Fear (1997).

"Do you consider yourself more Starbucks or D.D.?"

"D.D."

Leaving a female principal out of decision-making, unrepresented, while subjecting her to predators in her place of employment, while someone provides cover for these predators – might that strike anyone as gender discrimination, anyone female who has been raped on a rooftop?

This situation threatens financial suicide, by pretending to bring the potential to earn 3% plus my regular hourly rate in a commercial paper case. In this sand-grinding machine, men reserve the right to be aggressive defenders of men. Evans claims to have invented his popular tankless water heater design many years ago in his **mother's** garage. In my garage, for the past five years, somebody has been stacking propane gas tanks, leaving a bunch of junk, and, more recently, vandalizing my cars. *RE* as in RE for pay.

R informs me that he travels to Chicago business frequently. On one out-of-state sojourn, someone in Chicago sends me a computer disk, one not wanted or requested. The **Cleaner 3.0,** instructs its recipient to insert the disk inside my computer to make it run faster. Doing this allows third-party access to alter the computer such as adding, deleting, and reporting data to unknown third parties. The timing, origin, and purpose suggest a nefarious purpose emanating from the Chicago people who sent it to me.

It seems more like a passenger file disk, the sort of activity that probably relates to a whistleblower complaint vs. MELA, a group formed, according to its leadership, to "support the career advancement for plaintiff's attorneys." One of their leaders tells me that her "Sister is entering a "downward spiral." She recommends storing confidential documents on the Cloud storage on the trade groups' listserv.[53] Bandwidth on my internet access disappears. This part of the labyrinth might be Ursa minor where the serial killers front small sums of money, usurp areas in computers generally considered owned by the private business, then make extortionate claims that threaten the target's livelihood. Much like the experience of Navalny, a Russian attorney that ran against Vladimir Putin, who claims the FSB attempted to murder him by applying nerve agent to his underwear.[54] Navalny calls Putin "Vladimir, the underpants poisoner." Analogous to a dispute over an unusually expensive appellate brief.

Daedalus liquidates the value of the expectancy at replacement value, *aftermarket* parts not expectation damages by offering an exceedingly arbitrary number.

This sends the message that my work is replaceable, when in fact, there is no other attorney in Worcester County who tries FMLA matters to a jury. The one female attorney I am aware of stopped taking discrimination and retaliation matters because the work would put her out of business. Anyone waiting to get paid for over five or more years is going to have an extremely difficult time not going bankrupt. It is a slow and painful death.

As an anti-corruption activist, Alexei Navalny defines corruption, in its classical sense, as "the exploitation of an official position for personal gain."[55] All documentation relating to contracts connected with the state, its officials, or their relatives should be made public, even contracts run through attorneys, if connected to discrimination and retaliation to avoid the risk of corruption. Otherwise, wealthy, connected elites will bury their opponents using extortionate tactics that bear no relationship to the rule of law.

DEATH.

In 2019, a client signs an MOU resolving race discrimination and retaliation cases against two Partners hospitals, the first filed a 2016, *Jasey v. MGH* (*Jasey I*) and the second in 2018, *Jasey v. the Brigham* (*Jasey II*).[56] An attorney who did none of the written work, who never entered an appearance before the case settles; asks me to accept 13% instead of the 20% due under a written contract for services, a contract to which he is alien. Thirteen, a number with significance to the proceeding.

Four days later, summoned to be re-deposed a third time in an investigation into a nonexistent disability requested by an attorney for MGH. Once again, I have a letter on the State's Disability Evaluation Services (DES) letterhead signed by the state agency responsible for making official determinations about whether individuals are in fact disabled. This agency has already determined that according to at least two separate physicians who have examined me, one of them a psychologist, I am capable of performing my work competitively in my chosen field and have no disability. This unnecessary inquiry occurs after prevailing against MGH. Both times. The matter was dismissed without action.

If the legal profession genuinely seeks to destigmatize mental health treatment, a proxy of the defendant should not be allowed to weaponize it.

X.

Now, counsel, a defense attorney, sits with another attorney, someone named in an earlier MCAD claim. They recommend $130,000 less than the face value of an already completed contract.[57] There is only one attorney named as payee for legal services. She is female.

In a recognizable pattern, union-affiliated adversaries advance baseless claims of malpractice in order to claim money on a contract in which they are alien, bore none of the risk, and perform none of the written work. A debt of free labor, the best corn[58] from another does not accrue to a non-party --- upon sham claims of wrongdoing. It's a croc. The enforcers– who is protecting them, if not the Minotaur and what is their reward? Like the Per centages agreement between Stalin and Churchill,[59] or the agreement between the Nazis and the eugenicist's[60] this type of containment is based on a deal with the devil – in exchange for the containment of gender discrimination issues and related whistleblowing related to discrimination in and these men expect transactional immunity as a reward for their tactics. In the labyrinth, woman's rights issues get reduced to little more than entertainment.

Since when does a man who is alien to a written contract have any rights to the rightful owner's proceeds? Where is it written? *We Didn't Start the Fire*? The rule of law is not distributed via YouTube at 261 hertz. All of this tension cannot be over a measly $50,000. From my perspective, this is about the rule of law – what a female should reasonably expect to be paid, and why it is wrong for men who defend harassers to interfere with those rights by intimidation.

Speaking out about this practice is part of a healthy democracy.

In his book, *Profiles in Corruption*, Schweizer criticizes progressives, because progressive ideology relies on expansion of federal power – the swamp - to accomplish social goals, necessary social goals, such as the goal of eliminating racism. I favor Democratic unions. On the other hand, unions that use intimidation, covert sabotage, or 'send to Coventry' boycotts against peaceful dissenters should be banned. Attorneys should not need to hire bodyguards or go into hiding after settling retaliation cases. Due to the union issue, and the relationship of the attorneys to powerful political players, this might suggest the idea that federal power might lurk in the background of this seemingly inconsequential private contract matter to quell opposition.[61]

Classical liberals seek to limit federal power to avoid the risk of abuse. The question is the limit of federal power and the right to actually discuss the issues without being attacked, usurped, and eliminated from the workforce. In the movie *Spotlight*, Mitchell Garabedian's character, played by Stanley Tucci describes the undue influence of a mysterious invisible hand. Less than a week after working on a harassment case involving the attorney recommending a $130,000 fee discount, his partner applies to live next door, in my house. She claims to be going through a *terrible divorce* with a Judge. *What Judge?* When the partner from GE was not accepted as a tenant, another tenant moves in. Shortly thereafter, this new tenant installs a video camera and records videos on site without notice. They move.

Next, a sleeved tattooed tenant resembling the *Girl with the Dragon Tattoo* submits a rental application. This tenant attracts an unusual level of foot traffic. Get a tip these tenants are recording conversations next door. They are asked to leave. Continuous recording without a warrant does not serve the public, nor does it uphold a duty to uphold the Constitution. It serves the pervasive Nazi mentality that normalizes open-air electronic prisons for all Americans.

The next eighteen months the place remains empty, mainly due to the concern that my adversaries are lurking around waiting for an opportunity to send criminals to inhabit my residence. This emptiness due to overfishing, the kind of overfishing that occurs when the third parties sent to fish, themselves experience mortality and any benefit from their presence has reached a level where the stock biomass has negative marginal growth. For the tenants sent to fish around for information, their interests have been negatively affected (they were asked to move) and the landlord has lost total yield meaning the income from rents are less than it would be if the fish were allowed to grow. As this pattern unfolds, the use of 3rd party data vendors turns increasingly aggressive until it swallows the target's 4th Amendment rights whole. Neither side benefits, but there is one party walking away with the cream. Guess who.

Elect
GREG STILLSON
to the
**UNITED STATES
SENATE**

XI.

A raven-haired Italian spitfire darkens my door. She says her father on the Cape suffers a stroke, and now she is going through a divorce, like all the characters in this story. Gregory's application refers to a terribly inauthentic credit rating, the same number that identifies a Russian double agent in *The Americans*. Her words, "I know. It looks bad."

She works as a Director of Marketing, formerly for PUMA. Her application reflects an annual income identical to the recommended "discount" from my recently discharged attorney. Who sends these individuals to pose as tenants?[62] After eight o'clock at night, one week before Christmas, a box truck pulls up Cross Street bearing the logo *My Three Sons*. Three oversized sets of feet on the side of the truck appear to be walking all over...*something*. My residence, to the left, turns into a war zone shortly after this woman appears at my door. The feet may refer to stamping out the left, a political campaign originating with an agreement between the Italian fascists (the right) and the Nazis (Socialist party) in this curated deep-state amusement park. This campaign created to bolster the growth of the 4th Reich, grounded on the repression of civil liberties. Hello Ripley's.

Gregory's husband, Ryan drives a white Lincoln SUV with license plate *MR 4*. Right about then, Westlaw changes my attorney advertising to list me as a "Family Law" attorney, and then, alters the listing further to include "Criminal Appeals." Keep in mind, I am the only attorney in all of Worcester County that prosecutes discrimination and retaliation cases against the state's largest medical-defense complex, including by naming several local police Chiefs in discrimination cases. The bio I submitted for publication gets promptly replaced by a ghostwritten version, full of inaccuracies and the kind of biased trope I represent plaintiffs in fighting. For one thing, I have never handled family law matters or criminal appeals. Labyrinthine press operations and marketing people work in mysterious ways. Actually, maybe it is not so mysterious after all.

Shortly after Gregory moves in my mail begins getting redirected to her door, and large numbers of boxes began showing up at mine. Inauthentic looking fundraising mailers from my alma mater appear doctored. My laptop turns into the Minotaur's playground. I can no longer perform most online functions and am pushed offline for the next year. What else?

"Can you hear voices next door?" Does my tenant seek to inquire whether he presence coincides in a late onset case of schizophrenia? Or, possibly whether I overhear conversations with the man she calls her boss in gleeful conversations about an unmarked vehicle on Route 20? Clever Italian Dons have put on a bathrobe and successfully feigned mental illness; it is as tried and true a strategy as any. But I tell her I see nothing, hear nothing, know nothing. Why collaborate with someone promoting the 4th Reich?[63]

Before long, she begins staging marketing messages like dog feces that need to be picked up. Everywhere I go. Online, in the trash, in my mailbox, inside my door. A recognizable pattern. Planning my vacation, a car rental ad baits me to rent a white Mercedes, only to switch the car with….the exact same car and model as that white Lincoln driven by her husband, Ryan Gregory, a man with "Mr. 4" on his license plate. Returning home from Pompano Beach, now I find my car vandalized. A black leather glove, the right hand, *la mano Nero*,[64] sits on the gearshift. Image of a plane exploding in two left below the passenger seat. Fluids drained. Battery drained. Calipers cut. Car was in perfect working order right before leaving on vacation. Now completely pushed offline a mysterious computer entity tracks everything online I do or attempt to do. These events represent the presence of il Sindicato.

"You can still use apps," Gregory suggests. How thoughtful. Now tell me how to navigate the criminal harassment and logo feces all over the house.[65] Don't overdo ideology and keep people focusing on mindless distractions, and BAM!

During my vacation in Pompano Beach. a strange man by the name of Al creeps up offering to be a tour guide. The Minotaur himself? Al describes himself as a computer engineer formerly employed by *Boeing.* An I.T. guy. Emphasizes *b-ow* when pronouncing Boeing. His affected pronunciation mirrors an attorney's speech, with whom I had contact before vacation. He pronounces the name Barbara *B-ow.* The computerized criminal harassment on all my electronics, in and around my residence, and in and around my cars, both later vandalized echoes this encounter.

Following this meeting with Al, my operating system gets completely disabled, rendering my computer unusable because it no longer installs necessary updates. Coincidentally, the computer whose operating system gets corrupted is the computer purchased with proceeds from the sham litigation aimed at my office by Mr. Vans, whose wife is unrepresented. YouTube's automatic programming feeds tunes like:

> *Papa was a rolling stone*
> *Wherever he laid his hat*
> *Was his home*
> *And when he died*
> *All he left us was ALONE*[66]

Al and R.E., the man from the tankless water heater entity, share a few things in common. First of all, they are both in Pompano Beach at the same time, both engineers by trade. Al works the van, while R.E. slams doors across the hall from my room at the *Beachcomber Hotel* like he's filming a Chanel Égoïste commercial .[7]

Al claims to work for Boeing as a computer engineer for twenty years. Coincidentally, Al, the I.T. guy, and Nils the self-identified Nazi, were both German nationals, with distinctive German accents, both seemingly connected to the Brigham. Al tells me

---

[7] **Discounting the Word "No"** Refusing to accept rejection. de Becker, The Gift of Fear (1997)

that he has Russian friends. Al's reference to Russian friends coupled with these occurrences more than suggest a 'One hand washes the other' type of relationship. In the Nazi camps, leaders marked prisoners with a series of badges to track the pecking order. Violent criminals were assigned a green upside-down triangular shaped badge and were treated better than the other prisoners because they could be relied on to keep other prisoners in line.

This is overt harassing conduct. What possible motive would a computer engineer have to stalk me on vacation with R.E, a mechanical engineer from NU?[67] What might Al and his Russian friends be cooking up? Al's computer skills probably could point search navigation systems to find exactly this hotel. If so, why? There is nothing cool or socially redeeming about criminals harassing women on vacation, but that is exactly what these conjoined turds are all about.

Controlling the routes to and from one's online presence allows a stalker to control not just their choice of hotel, but quite literally their entire online life – the products they found online, the apartments, employment opportunities, and can easily manipulate and control their social media.

"Women in general should be very concerned about being sexually exploited by a psychopath in order to remain in employment. Psychopaths see sex only as a power trip/control mechanism…employees should be wary of this at all times if they work with a psychopath." [68] Algorithm[8] on Amazon recommends the purchase of shiny black goat antlers.

Al shows me this photo saved in his phone. Note the Satanic overtones.

STEP AWAY FROM THE GOAT AL[69]

[8] A hacker or cockroach on my computer logged in to the ABA web site under the login name **Alex Harrison(AH) during the writing of this book**. In employment discrimination litigation , the acronym AH generally refers to "alleged harasser." The last name Harrison might refer to George Harrison, the drummer for the Beatles. Alex, or Al, a computer engineer harassing me on vacation who has Russian friends.

By definition, someone engaging in this type of conduct cares about power and control. The constitutional rights of the targeted female do not exist for people such as this. Al wants to discuss sharing an apartment. *No, I do not wish to share anything with you.*

"Psychopaths are always on the lookout for people they can successfully mind-control.

In 2008, a study entitled *A Pawn by Any Other Name: Social Information Processing as a Function of Psychopathic Traits*...invented a group of fictional characters from photographs of men and women...participants with high levels of psychopathic traits demonstrated enhanced recognition for the **unhappy, unsuccessful female character** – the most vulnerable individual in the line-up of characters. Eventually, the victim learns over time to either stop speaking altogether without the psychopath present or becomes a mimic of the psychopath's viewpoints.

Either way, the mind of the victim has been subtly and perniciously reordered by the psychopath and the victim abdicates their natural ability for social interaction via one-on-one communication with others while the **psychopath assumes** the role as the victim's unofficial representative in public."[70]

Al invites me to a local hangout called the 'Rusty Hook.' It is too loud for me.[71] Rusty is the name of a former Chief of Police recently sentenced for baiting someone under the age of 14. All of the *Alias* characters so far share a similar point of view with regard to women. Al asks me to tell him what I think. In the Boston obscenity and censorship trial on the book, *Naked Lunch*, attorney Edward DeGrazia asks Norman Mailer about his thoughts, to which Mailer replies,

"Well, I think that I don't want to go to great length about what I think."

Hailing from Long Beach, in Orange County, California, Al states that he now works in real estate development.

"Where would your work or office actually be?"

"Boca Raton," Al replies.

"Do you have a business card?"

"Not on me."

"Where did you work today?"

"At the beach. I have two partners right now on this project." *My Three Sons*, Al, Robert and one more Ryan, who drives a white Lincoln. Whose three sons? – Waxman, my former boss. That might explain why I got dark gray Lincoln SUV. After disclosing his two partners, Al divulges a tale of wiring large sums of his ex-wife's earnings to his sister's family in Eastern Europe to,

"Fix the family estate." Who's the fixer, and is this a legal form of conversion therapy, and if so, when was it conceived? After providing an exceptionally detailed and unsolicited explanation as to why his Nav-a-ho wife would have consented to such an unfavorable loss of large sums of money, Al suggests sending his ex-wife's money to Eastern Europe led to a *terrible divorce.*

All he received in the break-up was a late model gray Honda Odyssey minivan. Al's van smells faintly like stale moth balls. [9]

"Do you have any photos of the projects you have worked on? Maybe your current project?"

---

[9] **Too many details**. If a person is lying they will add excessive details to make themselves sound more credible to their chosen victim. de Becker, *The Gift of Fear* (1997)

"Not with me." In his hands the latest iPhone, complete with a video camera, and not a single photo of his million-dollar real estate projects in Boca. Claims the woman he took the money from was Navajo, a "joke." Al depicts his intended victim as an Indian stereotype, an alcoholic. How cute.

Minutes earlier, Al claims that he rents an apartment two weeks ago on the Beach. At the same time, he also rents out a condo to several tenants in Long Beach. Al claims that he kept residing *inside the condo* with his tenants *after* renting it out to them. In addition, he wants to barter work for living space and move to Massachusetts – all within 15 minutes of meeting me. A reformulated AK-47 bounty-type weapon keeps re-insinuating itself in places it does not belong. Everyone I come into contact with seems to have the same *Alias* and a friendly relationship with *Russians*. Like a Mr. Anderson calling card.

Al Gordon, after refusing to accept a police report concerning wrongful access to credit data by another officer, directs other officers to search compartments inside my car. At the same time, while my credit files are being tampered with, another weird Al, Al Bergeron collects $1500 to create a web site. A.B. tells me that he is totally disabled, with no source of income, while driving a brand-new Nissan Rogue, feigning to be a web designer, and wearing a worn polyester navy blazer. While we are having coffee another plains clothes detective sits next to us listening in to our conversation about the web site Al is supposed to be building. His conversation promotes a motivational speaker, like the SNL skit about Matt Foley, a guy who lives in a van down by the river. It is not very often that the person who offers to create your web site offers to create a web site for $1500 and disappears without creating the web site. For most people, that is a sign he is not who says he is. Al is being protected while he spies on an anti-discrimination attorney who has named several local Chiefs of Police in civil rights cases.

Why do you think the local police protect this creep and harass the discrimination attorney? Minding my own business, at the beach, while looking at real estate, a computer engineer, also named Al approaches. Within 15 minutes of meeting me wants to perform work at my house. He wants to barter unspecified work in exchange for housing – inside my house in Westborough – sight unseen. In rapid succession, three weird Als. Right about then, my iPhone turns into a war zone. Who can I ask? Leninist policing makes it exceedingly difficult to believe the police are serving anything but Al. Coinciding with this strange encounter, an introduction to a woman with a luxury condo who works for *Microsoft*.

Looking a place to buy in Florida, a realtor, a tall man, well over six feet two who looks more like doubles working details as a bouncer shows me a place that accepts no pets. A large **H** in white on the throw pillows sitting on the couch, prominently appear **to** set the scene, almost like window dressing. H a universal symbol for hospital.

"It is probably nothing." Shouldn't there at least be a reason to eviscerate someone's privacy rights more than 'probably nothing'? How does a woman divorce an abusive husband who stalks electronically, watching everything by computer, abusing remotely? He probably wonders the same thing. Maybe he has already concluded a divorce would be too expensive. All of these Al characters - one cucaracha.

Al recounts stories of his Navajo love being in three serious car accidents. He supposes the accidents were all her fault. This man is supposedly speaking about,

"The love of his life."

"Weren't you concerned about her?" Al replies no, he was not.

"Were you present at any of the accidents?"

"No," Al replies. Al claims that after the third accident, his Navajo wife was jailed for DUI. With a big smile, Al says he was enjoying reminiscing about his "Navajo girlfriend."

"Thinking of her reminds me of squash."

"Why is that?"

"That is what I am having for dinner."

"You really have a big problem with women who earn more money than you do, Al." Why would this man be harassing me on vacation one month after settling a case with MGH and the Brigham? Al insists,

"Judge what's her face was just pulled over for drunk driving...right around here." He gestures as if it had just happened in the neighborhood where we were sitting.

A dark-haired woman with blue eyes, in her early-to-mid 40's wearing a pinkish velour tracksuit, about the same height and weight as me sits in the aisle seat, blocking me on the airplane ride to the beach.. The woman introduces herself as Michelle from Gardner, MA, also known as *Chair City*. Michelle says she works as an autism counselor, helping autistic persons with personal hygiene issues. All of that sounds exceedingly gaslightingly specific.

"Let's hope everyone on the plane showered today."

"No problems with that here," Michelle opens her phone and displays grainy stock photos of a man she calls her boyfriend. She proudly describes him as Dutch. She shows me what she suggests representing "before" and "after" photos during her online relationship with the Dutch boyfriend, a man she has never met, who is the love of her life, now dead. Michelle describes a Dutch man living at home with his mother who never worked a day in his life. She said he did not need to work because he was from a wealthy family. In the before photo, he was smiling and looked clean-shaven. She also claimed that over the course of an online-only relationship with him she observed his health severely deteriorate. In the after photo, he appeared to have experienced a shattering loss. The man in the image had a scraggly beard and appeared disheveled with a vacant look in his eyes. He looked how someone might expect a street person to look. The man appeared to be on death's door. The before and after montage, here staged in more of a gaslighting type of warning of death. Continuing her story, Michelle claims that her Dutch boyfriend recently committed suicide. She recounts details of the man's emotional turmoil with an unusual amount of relish.

Michelle smiles, "I hope I pass the test." In *Commonwealth v. Carter*, a juvenile court holds a defendant, also named Michelle, like my extremely strange seat-mate next to me on my flight to Florida in February 2020, guilty of involuntary manslaughter for encouraging her long-distance boyfriend, Conrad Roy, to commit suicide. *Verdict, Commonwealth v. Carter, No. 15YO0001NE (Mass. Juv. Ct. June 16, 2017)* This stranger is actually bragging about encouraging her online boyfriend to kill himself. A woman who provides mental health services to vulnerable people in Massachusetts. A Facebook whistleblower testifies before Congress as dangerous algorithms contribute to the public health crisis regarding mental health. Out of the virtual stalking world, algorithm joins forces with Michelle, a live proxy stalker bragging about inflicting mental anguish to the extent that she actually causes the death on someone in her social media network she calls her boyfriend. *Hello psychopath next door.*

"Are you *Irish?*" she smiles.

"What's the right answer?" The appearance of this disturbed individual raises the question. No respectable person would get involved in this type of conduct. Just the thought that there are people involved in this conduct is sickening. Even as a joke it is so unbelievably lame, so far beyond the realm of respectable conduct only someone extremely disturbed would participate. If you have to explain to someone why gaslighting a complete stranger on an airplane with jokes about causing online suicide is wrong, this is a prima facie case of psychopath - not a case of bad parenting, the person involved is disturbed. Yet, this appears to be connected to all the other characters in this script. Totally disgusting.

"I am *Irish*,"[72] Michelle in the pinkish velour tracksuit continues, "and I love my *boss.*" In *Commonwealth v. Carter*, 481 Mass. 352, 115 N.E.3d 559 (2019) the defendant used electronic communication to encourage her boyfriend to commit suicide. The case tests the limits of criminal behavior and accountability for that behavior. Seated next to me on the plane to Pompano Beach is a woman interested in testing these boundaries, or, at least, telling a tale of her wanton experience of doing this to another human being. Is this a right-wing propaganda campaign protected by the First Amendment, or something intending to push its target to commit suicide?

It is not an ethical use of your training as an attorney to participate in conduct that might injure or cause the death of a third-party. If there is a medical provider involved in this type of conduct it is equally unethical. Michelle works as a marionette on behalf of a silent partner, a health care provider testing whether encouraging online suicide passes a legal test. Who sent her to wear this pink velous tracksuit costume? It is a costume cut from the same cloth as the Nav-a-ho script written for Al the goat molester. A man who sounds an awful lot lile an attorney with whom I had contact immediately before my vacation.

"Do the Dutch and the Irish get along well?" I half-joke. Michelle, road agent number two, says her Dutch boyfriend's suicide occurred recently, just one month before the flight in February 2019. Michelle tells me that one day she logs into her computer and her Dutch boyfriend was not there. Eventually, she says she realizes that he was dead. Where did Michelle, or anyone for that matter, get such a delightful suicide story?

Michelle insists the death was caused by excessive alcohol consumption, not a Dutch door mishap. Other than grainy stock photos there was not a lot to go on. Rhymes with Hell seems a lot more like the kind of person who didn't break for small animals crossing the street. She sped up.

"It just is a lot of money." I have never met this woman before in my life. She has dark reddish hair, fair skin, a velour pink tracksuit, and wants to talk about her "Dutch boyfriend's suicide" What business does she have really? Rhymes with Hell invites me to join her social media network.

"If you were part of my social network I would write you every day." Michelle, as charming an invitation as that sounds, I think no. I do not want to be put in an early grave with your YouTube Gaslighting or sock puppet accounts sent to destroy my privacy and social contacts. Rhymes with Hell proceeds to tells me that she has plans to travel to see the,

"Dead boyfriend's mother" and repeat her *classy* "Dutch Suicide" monologues at the boyfriend's mother's home. The mother? You must mean the person hoped to *diss-in-her-it* the target with this Coventry styled predation.

Upon arrival at Fort Lauderdale International Airport Rhymes with Hell, tells me she is going to Selma, Georgia. **Selma?** These 3rd party data vendors are not so subtle. "You went 2000 miles out of your way on a flight with a five-hour layover? Why not just fly direct to Georgia?"

"I just love to travel." A mental health counselor *causing mental anguish. Encouraging suicide.* "This sadistic agenda was very popular in the 1960's and 1970's when the term 'being sent to Coventry' became kind of a code word to socially isolate individuals within a factory or other working environment. According to the O.E.D. the first usage of this expression occurs in 1647. The ultimate aim would be to get the isolated individual to commit suicide, which tragically did happen in countless cases. In many cases, this inhumane tactic was fully endorsed and actively encouraged by trade union leadership in order to copper-fasten union members into an "Us and them" mentality.[73] Send to Coventry campaigns also bears a close relationship to boycotting, where a boycott intends to focus on the rights or actions of women. "Secondary boycotts" directly interfering with vendors relied upon for maintenance of a business may not be legal in some states. It is the kind of campaign someone knowledgeable in union boycotts might know how to organize.

Al's mouth with that VanDyke beard is still moving. Now he is talking about hiring him so that he can move to Massachusetts and barter free rent, while he works for the psychopath grid's Suicide Hit Squad. The tankless water heating alliance sent their most fact-repellent troll. Al sits to my left showing me another photo of the dark-haired woman he claims to be his former Navajo Indian wife.

"She lives right around here." Showing me a stock photo, he takes a picture of me, and compares the two, his face letdown when the two photos do not actually look alike. He closes his phone.[74] Continuing his script, his wife had been arrested for DWI. He made a number of other claims about this woman while loudly slurping vanilla ice cream and shots of Jägermeister. What's next in the tired old script Al, a thrilling discussion on the importance of recycling steel? Between SpongeBob, Rhymes with Hell, and the three Als, what are these suicide trolls cooking up? More conversion therapy and manufactured shampoo for the unwilling? A revenge of the nerds anarchist cookbook, *The International Sled-Dog's Guide to Manufacturing Shampoo*. The Beachcomber Hotel is just ten-minute ride. On the way back to the hotel, Al drives in circles around a city block with a pink neon HOTEL sign for the next hour. The letters T-E-L were completely blacked out.

The sign says HO in bright white light. checked his radio and set it to 93.7 FM.

Al,[3] a super malignant species of Hohenschönhausen troll on Mexican steroids no one has created a vaccine for yet is studying my face for any reaction. One cure for this viral troll species – individual liability for cyberstalking and intrusions into U.S. citizen's Constitutional rights.[75] Until then, a kick in his high-ranking Leninist balls would be therapeutic for one of us.

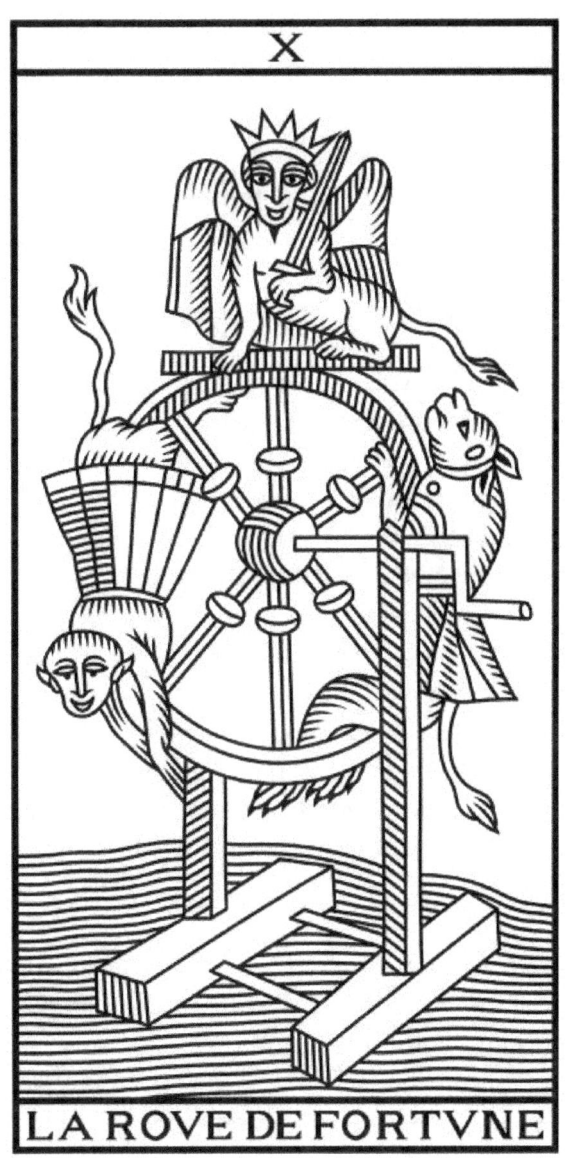

XII.

At home, neighborhood activity signals the presence of shady political operatives. Either that, or my neighborhood recently relocated to a border town. The most remarkable intensity of street theatre. Campaigns around Westborough in 2020 evidence little political canvassing, with the exception of a pleasant married woman who works at the Town library. No political banners on cars. No canvassers approach me at my home. Just a lot of noise. No political banners. No peaceful demonstrations. Exhaust. Noise. Honking. The neighbors at A horse stands in the tall grass off Route 30 ready for a Klan rally. The horse wears a costume with imperial wizard headdress reminiscent of the death card. It's not Halloween.

Neighborhood traffic patterns include unusual street theater, staging of parked cars with noticeable tradecraft, and noise disturbances by cars with rigged mufflers creating excessive exhaust, vandalism, and criminal harassment by various trucks sandwiching me in everywhere I go. Someone should really tell MR 4 to Midasize it. Municipal vehicles blocking access to roads, arbitrarily parked to block my driveway, my street, or common routes to shopping. Staged activism occurs, largely involving municipal vehicles and off-duty police officers in trucks, frequently trucks with *Johnson Controls* insignia. What could these truck drivers possibly trying to say? It's a mystery.

Biden and Harris seem to have tremendous groundswell of local support, observable in the signage posted within the 495-corridor leading towards Cape Cod. One noteworthy non-political campaign, 13 Ruggles Street fill their front yard with Flamingoes and invite passersby to honk their horns in celebration of their sons 13th birthday. Signage changes frequently from one commercial enterprise to another. I could not help but wonder why there would be the need for such an aggressive form of.....whatever this is. What is this really? A new exclusion for *Insurrection* on a private residential insurance policy strikes as more than a little unusual. Why would that be necessary?

During the Spring of 2019 and continuing into 2020, both of my cars were vandalized. One of the cars has its calipers cut, fluids bled, and battery drained by leaving the dome light in the on position so that the car would not start. A black leather glove, not mine, left positioned over the gearshift. Below the passenger seat, on the floor, to the right side sits a crumpled image depicting a plane exploding in two, crashing mid-air. My snow removal guy removes half the snow needed to get around the yard, then tells me someone already paid him. His name: Nick Licata.. Custom made to appear to be caused by ZPU-2 anti-aircraft gun *Subtle*.

Would your average American feel comfortable exercising their First Amendment rights if they knew that their personal property would be vandalized, unregistered lobbyists would conduct rallies in front of their home, and they would be facing a tidal wave criminal harassment with no genuine political message other than to disturb the peace?

Anyone hiring a third-party troll to pose and harass someone as a Michelle Carter look alike, has more than a few issues. Viewed through the lens of a notorious 19th century case, and the Michelle Carter case, the facts present the classic case of going for the jugular. The word is **vicious**. One way the powerful keep the less wealthy or politically connected in a constant state of imminent threat, is the perpetual reminder that in times of food scarcity, it is the weaker and more vulnerable become food sources for apex predators.

This famous English common law case, *R v Dudley and Stephens* (1884) 14 QBD 273 DC establishes that in a case of survival cannibalism, necessity cannot be a defense to murder. The case goes like this. On July 23 or 24, while Parker (P), a shipmate languishes in a coma, his shipmates debate whether it was better that one of them die so that the others survive. The drew lots. Brooks (B) refuses. That night, Dudley (D) again raises the matter with Stephens (S). *D* and *S*, with wives and families, determine, therefore, it would be inconsequential for P to die. They wait until morning. No prospect of rescue in sight, D and S silently signal to kill P. Killing P before his natural death would mean blood to drink. B, who had not been party to the earlier discussion, claims to have signaled neither assent nor protest. D always insists that B assents. S stands by to hold the youth's legs down if he struggles. D pushes his penknife into Parker's jugular vein, killing him. The Crown holds D and S responsible for murder and sentences each of them to the statutory death penalty.

On July 23, an unmarked dark gray State Police vehicle pulls me over on Route 20, 20 feet from a Penske truck rental. The state police officer jokes he would not want to "Take anything that does not belong to him." The day before the false stop, Mr. 4's wife, Gregory, a *Director of Marketing*, hands me an escheatment letter dated July 22 originating from

Dallas. Gregory's appearance, far from Aryan, short, dark, and with a club-like foot prosthesis, suggests a role akin to Joseph Goebbels, a man whose propaganda campaigns during WWII fed the Nazi war machine based on the master race theory.[76]

Escheatment[77] generally means the government owes the addressee money. The escheatment letter originates from Dallas, TX. Following a request for more information, no reply at all.

The July 22 escheatment letter, without providing details about the subject-matter of the property in question, contains a request for indemnification. It does not specify the terms of the indemnification, rather, in exchange for a duty to pay money the letter acknowledges is already owed, it demands a blanket signature agreeing to reimburse the holder for an unspecified indemnity.

Indemnification[78] often means reimbursement of unlimited attorney's fees. The letter seeks agreement to pay unlimited attorney's fees in exchange for the issuance of a check the letter admits is already owed. This is called lack of consideration. Who does this letter intend to indemnify, if not the police actors seeking to be rewarded with attorneys to defend their willful indifference?

In order for a contract to be enforceable, there must be consideration. Demanding something *nicer* in return than what was already owed, this is a corrupt practice promoted by people who simply want payment for what does not belong to them.

When the ticket for the false State Police stop on July 23 gets reversed, the DMV sends a letter signed by Jaime T' Esler. How improbable is it for a former client with the last name *Esler*, to have a relative with a cannibalized Ellis Island version of the same last name Jaime *T'Esler* who heads up the DMV? The letter requesting indemnification is a lot like Britney refusing to pay her father to hire attorneys to defend his abuse. It is a scam.

A thick white smoke blusters out of the engine of the car. Thickly covering the windows making it was impossible to see cars in front of me or to the left. My mechanic sees a brand-new clamp at the end of what appears to be a forcibly removed hose. The mechanic tells me it looks more than a little suspicious. There could be no other reasonable explanation other than vandalism.

The next week, someone removes the rear brake light. Then, the car's rear-view mirror was broken. Next, the rear gate bent so that it would not close properly. The last time the get bent treatment surfaced it someone politically connected looking for an extrajudicial do-over.

Municipal vehicles block my street. Large CAT vehicles back in and out of my driveway for no apparent reason. Underground grid opens up and signs of manipulation appear. Electronic harassment repeatedly coded to the number 66[79], seemingly intended to relate to D-Day, more in the sense of promoting propaganda related to a *Master*. Aggressive vehicles sandwich me in, traveling to my family house and back, all over Worcester County. If I pull over on the way to a grocery store to let Frank's Appliances box truck following too close go by, within minutes, more hostile convoy bookends return. Through the local Town school zone, on route to the post office, police pull in front and behind my car. Isn't there more important police business than harassing a discrimination attorney who recently settled a case with Mass General and the Brigham?

When the car bookends are not police vehicles, and non-state actors sandwich my car in, the license plate covers display

DAN's JEEP

At the last visit to the place where I have been taking my car for the last fifteen years a noticeable change. A place operated by a local family with whom I entrusted my car without question for the past fifteen years has been taken over by extraterrestrials. He tells me he, "Wants to make sure my gas cap is on."

This statement coincides with signal......programming...G-A-S...G-A-S...G-A-S....G-A-S.....G-A-S .....

C-A-P ... C-A-P ..... C-A-P ...

G-A-S...G-A-S...G-A-S....

C-A-P ... C-A-P ..... C-A-P ...next the light to indicate the deflated tires.

When the Nazis chose to use radios as the primary mode of propaganda they knew that it would reach into the minds of their targets more so than other available forms of communication. A form of electronic terrorism, where the goal is to intimidate into an unthinking type of conformity, so that <u>before</u> you exercise the right to object, your resources have been completely depleted and you are in a receptive state of compliance. The most effective way to directly reach into a target's psyche while ensuring that they will keep quiet about the abuse is to scare them into thinking that if this is bad now, speaking out about it will make things worse. It is common knowledge by now, today's electronic vehicles are susceptible to hacking. When you have been targeted by someone resembling Gene HACKMAN and that person tells you that he identifies with the Nazi party, beware.

The mechanic who repairs the vandalism shrugs his shoulders as if to say, you could bring your car back here, but why would you want to do that? The repair had nothing to do with a gas cap. It had to do with vandalism. It appears that he has been offered cover by the resident Nazis. Vandalism that cost more than $1000 to fix. The pattern of vandalism aimed at both my cars continues in a never-ending pattern

The Nazis viewed their targets as valueless. They targeted non-Nazis, and step-by-step, measure by measure took, discounted, and denigrated them until the word *valueless* was on fact true.

The goal, to usurp property or civil rights from those deemed less valuable to their cause and turn it over to the masters. Inherent in this idea, the need to blame the target as *damaged goods* when in fact the source of the damage is the underground Zersetzung agents. This is how the Nazis used mental illness to frame their victims as damaged goods and take what did not belong to them. This behavior by a paramilitary volunteer bent on revenge, revenge based on attacking a woman on the road so that he can damage her car and get money has its roots in conduct sanctioned by Nazis. The vandalizer wants others to believe this is honorable.

Outside the repair ship, a car sits parked near my vehicle with a U.S. Official plate, exceedingly rusted. The Department of Transportation or DOT is the agency responsible for the removal of roadkill, sometimes in connection with animal control officials. Under the Driver Privacy Act of 2015, S 766, emergency doctors and the DOT have the right to access a drivers black box in cases related to public safety.[80] Throughout 2019-2020, dead raccoons positioned near my home, en route past Walbridge

Road, and at the entrance to the street at my mother's home. In at least one case, the animal positioned near Harvey waste removal, left half alive and was suffering and needed to be moved to avoid being hit by oncoming traffic. Anyone posing dead (or dying) animals is likely disturbed. The frequency of their appearance, the position, and location suggest staging and not random animal mortality. "Acts of cruelty to animals are not mere indications of a minor personality flaw in the abuser; they are symptomatic of a deep mental disturbance. Research in psychology and criminology shows that people who commit acts of cruelty to animals don't stop there—many of them move on to their fellow humans. Murderers … very often start out by killing and torturing animals as kids," says Robert K. Ressler, who developed profiles of serial killers for the Federal Bureau of Investigation (FBI)"[81]

My home entered when I was not home, despite locking all the doors and windows, my possessions repositioned, electronics settings changed, books left open to passages that suited these predators arguments. In the attic, a RATT album positioned to be discovered with the hit "Don't Bite the Hand That Feeds," and a second album called the "Jim and Ingrid Jim Croce album." Neither one of these albums belong to me or any of the previous tenants.[82]

The tidal wave of misconduct has little to do with state security or public safety and more to do with police corruption. These state police functions effect to intimidate and neutralize whistleblower activity. Advocates for employees who charge MGH and the Brigham, without question the largest hospital employer in the state, with retaliation against its employees and their witnesses should not be neutralized by using the state police power. The rain of cash flowing from a wealthy entity like MGH, and the Brigham can powerfully influence people to do things good people would never consider.

In a polarized political environment, whistleblowers do not necessarily fit a clear purpose. In Leninist Russia, such people were sent to gulags, and murdered. On the heels of a contested employment issue with MGH's employees, their representatives have requested investigations into my mental health; this is much the same when opposing the political elite in Russia. This is a hallmark of anti-democratic regimes with little tolerance for criticism of its officials.

XIII.

It is April 7. A rigged rumbling muffler right out of a Ghost Square Hammer video pulls aggressively in front of my car at the Burger King drive thru in Shrewsbury. On the plate two identifiable letters read BC. *Before Christ? Bain & Company?* A silver economy hatchback. A Ford Focus. *Concentrate.* A message conveyed through the window from the *Freikorp* that "Someone just purchased you an 'Ultra Crispy Chicken Sandwich,'" The driver blocks me in, for a few minutes, signaling yet another crucifixion on the horizon. On the drive past the Worcester Airport, the Rolling Stones song, *Sympathy for the Devil* plays on the radio.

"These may be shades, who go unknotting what their debts have tied."[83] Two white men are seated in the driver and passenger seats. On the back rear window, someone prominently positions an ACTON decal on the lower left side. Lord Acton, best known for the remark,

"Power tends to corrupt, and absolute power corrupts absolutely. Great men are almost always bad men..." A short period of time later, a continuous wave emanates from a vehicle parked overnight in an adjacent parking lot next to Saint Luke's Catholic Church, pointing at the attic. A ringing or zapping noise slowly increases. CW can cause permanent injury or death in higher frequency pulsed attacks.[84] After leaving this location, the wave attack travels to another family residence, suggesting it is not the location, but something else. A helicopter flies overhead. The vehicle appears to contain non-state actors. The timing, the circumstances surrounding a substantial discrimination settlement against MGH suggests retaliation by someone known to me. In 2019, where the victim to offender relationship could be identified, 1479 of 1622 homicide victims were killed by a someone they knew.[85]

Stanley Milgram sought to determine whether there is an innate "Nazi" character. For four dollars for an hour of their time, individuals pose as quasi-medical authority figures in white coats. They asked these test subjects to increase electrical currents to 450 volts to shock subjects in adjacent rooms upon command. Even when warned that doing so could result in permanent injury or death, 26 of 40 test subjects, or 65% complied. Results suggest that complete strangers will do inherently evil acts for as little as four dollars an hour. Robert Jay Lifton's work studies the Nazi doctors during WWII, in situations where informed consent can never be obtained. Lifton explains Nazi doctors as the forming of two distinct personalities. The first personality faces the world and plays the family person who claims a position of virtue above that of the abused. The second face is the one who abuses. Lifton theorizes that doubling, allows the second face to reinforce a political power structure. The usurper.

IT'S SHOWTIME

U.S. Government officials attribute *Havana Syndrome* to attacks from Russian operatives as the likely culprit,[86] however, psychotronic technology has been available for use since 1952, and over the past 69 years has likely found its way to commercial markets. The message sent from the Ford Focus driver, that he purchased me "an ultra-crispy fried chicken sandwich," suggests a commercially available weapon. After moving to avoid this assault, a helicopter files overhead, at a relative's home, and a continuing pattern ensues. The law does not recognize consent to assault or consent to criminal harassment, however it does acknowledge that in cases where women are attempting to leave abusive relationships or situations they are most vulnerable to attack. Generally, this abuse comes from someone they know.

The NASEM study identifies, "the sudden onset of a perceived loud sound, sensation of perceived pressure or intense vibration in the head, and pain in the ear or more diffusely in the head." Wave energy operates like a remote electronic egg scrambler for the human brain. Pulsed radiofrequency RF attacks often result in symptoms such as dizziness, headache, fatigue, anxiety, memory loss, and cognitive defects. [10] *See, Plausible Mechanisms. (Citations omitted).* Pulsing may be the most important factor in determining the biological effects of low-intensity continuous wave (CW) energy weapons that operate under frequencies between 2.05-250 GHz. *(Pakhomov and Murphy, 2000; Adams and Williams, 1976)* Studies comparing CW with pulsed wave weapons suggest that while both negatively affect targets, pulsed energy results in more serious and permanent injury, e.g., Transformer Energized Megavolt Pulsed Output (TEMPO) "observed a negative effect on cognitive function in rats," according to one study, deleterious effects include "time perception and discrimination tasks." *(Raslear et. Al. 1993)*

---

[10] National Academies of Sciences, Engineering and Medicine, 2020, *An Assessment of Illness in US Government Employees and Their Families at Oversees Embassies*, Washington, DC, The National Academies Press.

The timing of the attack, concurrent with a pattern of criminal harassment aimed at my house, vandalism of personal property, and intimidation directly interfering with the exercise of civil liberties, including the reporting of this crime to authorities suggests coordination with a wealthy and politically connected entity.

The mechanism contains a unique signature. As an acquired brain injury tool (**ABIT**) by definition it is intended to be used to inflict injury. Studies report persistent postural-perceptual dizziness (**PPPD**) "'Weaponry based on new physics principles: direct energy weapons, geophysical weapons, wave-energy weapons, genetic weapons, psychotronic weapons, etc., is part of the state arms procurement program for 2011-2020,' the Russian defense minister reported to President Putin in March 2012. For the layperson, uninformed of secret military research, this sounds like science fiction. But it is not fiction." [*Assassins*, page xiv.]

Data culled from confidential listserv surveys suggests that slightly more than 50% of targets are required to undergo involuntary incarceration in psychiatric hospitals as a direct result of attack with CW weapons.[87] If you are a betting type of person interested in weaponization of wave energy weapons to accomplish a certain goal, this statistic likely weighs into its cost-to-benefit analysis.

Cui bono? Someone interested in repression that involves psychiatric imprisonment. Psychopaths are well known to orchestrate situations that they themselves would fear the most. In addition to investigating situations by looking at a target's inner circle and working out, this is another telltale sign about who was involved in this criminal activity. By now, an easily recognizable motive suggests a deliberate choice to use this mechanism, because it advances a specific and consistent agenda – an attempt to eliminate a competitor from the marketplace by use of a fabricated pretext. This pretext is the unnecessary investigation of a non-existent disability. Even without details, all their patterns are consistent

In *Puzzling People*, Thomas Sheridan cites an Air Force Study regarding RTPJ in which researchers found that test subjects were more likely to judge actions solely on the basis of whether they resulted in suffering, and not whether electromagnetic harassment was morally wrong in and of itself.

BUT DID
YOU DIE

A labyrinthian influence campaign surrounding the *Ultra Crispy* psy**hot**ronic attack suggests promoters subscribe to the idea that use of such attacks should be excused provided death is not the result. This idea, by definition, emanates from the point of view that morality does not matter. This is the essence of psychopathy.

Under the *Declaration of Human Rights*, the *Convention Against Torture*, and the *Convention on the Elimination of Discrimination Against Women (CEDAW) a treaty adopted by the UN in 1979*, the use of psychotronic weapons or continuous wave (CW) energy weapons is inhumane. These attacks are crimes against humanity.

In these uncertain times, wealthy Americans have been upping their security, using private security, and building private safe rooms in their homes. **HR 2977** the law prohibiting the use of Directed Energy Weapons prohibits their use within sixty kilometers above a private residence's airspace. Short of banning these weapons altogether, enhanced protections from the use of psychotronic or wave energy weapons on American soil against private citizens is necessary.

Without enhanced protections, opportunistic predators likely can find these weapons commercially and use them to directly attack democracy. Even the threat of their use directly interferes with the exercise of civil liberties. There are online groups of targeted individuals who quite literally fear for their lives and liberty as a result of these weapons. [88]

This is not a free America.

Biden U.N speech to the 76th Congress of the U.N..: *As new technologies continue to evolve, we'll work together with our democratic partners to ensure that new advances in areas from biotechnology to quantum computing, 5G, artificial intelligence and more are used to lift people up, to solve problems and advance human freedom — not to suppress dissent or target minority communities.* But the mission must be clear and achievable, undertaken **with the informed consent of the American people** and, whenever possible, in partnership with our Allies. U.S. military power must be our tool of last resort, not our first, and it should not be used as an answer to every problem we see around the world.

If *Bain and Company, A Consulting Firm Too Hot To Handle*, accurately depicts a company rife with conflicts at the heart of several important cases of corruption, the foregoing events reasonably raise questions about the weaponization of data vendors who usurp 4th Amendment rights, and the use of local police by wealthy and politically connected hospital defendants to engage in acts of repression more than likely to interfere with the exercise of civil liberties. This represents a direct attack on democracy. In my last contact, Gregory states the *"Roads are too Ho-T,"* referring to the fact that the roads were not safe due to the aggressive caravans of cars and box truck car sandwiches blocking the normal flow of traffic from Westborough to Paxton. This was an extremely well-organized operation.

XIV.

Far away, jettisoned out of state, underneath the tropical sunshine two strangers approach.

"We're from the Jewish Mafia" The wife, a retired manager of a British Charm School, expresses fascination with Vietnam. During Vietnam, the Johnson administration employs doublespeak to excuse its conduct and to get out of the war. This man bears a message from the other side. A wealth of information, as rich as the Sierra Madre.

"Do you like my hat?" Atop his lovely wife's head of short white hair sits a khaki Mao hat. Khaki rhymes with shacky. Talks about her friend named Mary a holocaust survivor she calls every Sunday. She describes herself as a helicopter parent. Talking up her son **Al**ex, now married and in his 40s, she glows with pride describing his Alpha group activities, such as his fondness for an expensive Alpha Romeo vehicle, wearing Stetson cowboy hats, and the 50 Shades of Gray series of novels. Stetson, the name of an attorney involved in collection matters, affiliated with Consigli Construction. We talk about films.

"Have you seen any of the *Shades of Gray* movies?" It is not really my kind of movie. Both of Madonna's criticisms were right, it is not romantic, and no one eats p——- that much.

"Once Upon a Time in Hollywood, a Quentin Tarantino film is another good one,*"* the woman insists. That movie involves a woman being blowtorched to death in a swimming pool. How charming. I can see why her son does not want to be in the same state as she is in. I have never met anyone that feigns friendship while texting her adult son all day long with a play-by-play of events by the pool in real-time. Stressing she "could be vicious," on cue, a physically disabled man by the name of Billy Harrington enters, stage left. Calling me over to where he is seated, the man suggests an online search for one of my recent defendants' hospitals. Glued to her tablet, wearing sunglasses, the woman tells me she believes in the importance of,

"Making the disabled not feel invisible," Here we go again. In Leninist versions of the truth, quality varnish can be the difference between winning and losing, and we are in for more Linear B script.

"Hello Billy! How are you doing today? It is so nice to see you. What a beautiful day to be outside." They engage in pleasantries until the poolside pavers burn the soles of her feet. She retreats in search of flip flops. The man's wife describes herself as a helicopter parent. Turning to me, she whispers, conspiratorially,

"Yesterday Billy told me that he thinks he had an accident surfing. That is not how he injured himself at all. He told me something completely different the day before. Tomorrow he will probably say something different again. He does not remember what really happened to him." *Definitely not a wave.*

"It was *not* a surfing accident," emphatically, "Ask him how he injured himself the next time you see him, he will tell you something different from surfing." *A particle.*

The husband lays down on a chair to the left of me. The wife to the right. Like a sandwich.

"They should pay for what they did to you." A silent bystander, does he see the police, jury, and executioner all as one?

"When our son moved into his apartment at school Walmart had this fried chicken. ….. It was irresistible."

The man continues, "You beat them....they are not attorneys." In reference to Islam, "If they are dealing with a non-believer, the follower of Muhammed is allowed to lie."

"Strange religion." The wife tells me, "I prefer Matthew McConaughey. My sister was not as popular as I was. I married early and lived the life. Compared to my sister, who had a miserable divorce, I have been happy. While she was stuck in England, I was here, being the 'Toast of the Town!'" [89] A bit like the John Waters film *Cecil B. Demented.* about an A-list actress who gets kidnapped and forced to be in a B-movie.

"Don't feel abandoned, now, Margaret…."

City dwellers habituated to the sound of fog horns in the night know that they no longer have any utility. For the tourists, fog horns and the ringing of the trolley cars provide musical accompaniment to the cacophony. Buffalo Bill stopped making appearances after they left environs the *Shushing Woman.*

Acknowledgements

I would like to thank the many people who contributed to the writing of this book. Thanks to my family and friends who have supported me over the years. To those people with whom I lost touch, I am also thankful for the time spent with you.

I would also like to thank the many psychopaths who have crossed my path over the years. All of you have played an invaluable part in realizing this book.

WORKS CITED

Black, Edwin, IBM and the Holocaust, Crown Publishers, New York (2001)

Brady v. Maryland, 373 U.S. 38 (1963)

Citizens United v. Federal Election Commission, 558 U.S. 310 (2010)

Commonwealth v. Carter, No. 15YO0001NE (Mass. Juv. Ct. June 16, 2017)

Corson, William R. and Crowley, Robert T., The New KGB, Engine of Soviet Power, Quill William Morrow, New York ((1985)

Davis, Lanny, Scandal: How "Gotcha" Politics is Destroying America, Palgrave McMillan, New York (2006)

El-Hai, Jack, The Nazi and the Psychiatrist, *Herman Göring, Dr. Douglas M. Keller, and a Fatal Meeting of the Minds at the End of WWII* (2013)

Farrow, Ronan, Catch and Kill Lies, Spies & a Conspiracy to Protect Predators Little, Brown & Company (2019)

Fitzpatrick, Robert L. Ponzinomics, The Untold Story of Multi-Level Marketing, Fitzpatrick Management, Inc., Charlotte, North Carolina (2020)

Forwood, A.K., Gang-Stalking and Mind-Control, The Destruction of Society Through Community Spying Networks, Lulu Publishing (2011)

In the Matter of Amway Corporation, Inc., et al. 93 F.T.C. 618 (May 8, 1979) (Available on the FTC web site at: https://www.ftc.gov/sites/default/files/documents/commission_decision_volumes/volume-

93/ftc volume decision 93 january - june 1979pages 618-738.pdf)

Limone v. United States, 497 F. Supp. 2d 143 (D. Mass. 2007)

Pacepa, Ion Mihai, Red Horizons, Regnery Gateway, Washington D.C. (1987)

Pacepa, Ion Mihai and Rychlak, Ronald, Disinformation, WND Books, Washington D.C. (2013)

Paine, Thomas, Common Sense, Coventry House Publishing, Columbia, SC (D. 1776, copyright 2016)

Rid, Thomas, Active Measures: The Secret History of Disinformation and Political Warfare, Farrar, Strauss &;;amp; Giroux, New York (2020)

Schweizer, Peter, Extortion: How Politicians Extract Your Money, Buy Votes, And Line Their Pockets, Houghton Mifflin Harcourt, Boston (2013)

Schweizer, Peter, Profiles in Corruption: Abuse of Power by America's Politically Elite, Harper Collins Publishers, New York (2020)

Snyder, Alvin A., Warriors of Disinformation American Propaganda, Soviet Lies, and the Winning of the Cold War, An Insider's Account, Arcade Publishing, New York (1995)

Stent, Angela, Putin's World, Hachette Book Group, New York (2019)

Sudoplatov, Pavel and Anatoli, with Jerrold L. and Leona Schecter, Special Tasks, The Memoirs of an Unwanted Witness – A Soviet Spymaster, Little Brown & Company, Boston ((1995)

Volodarsky, Boris, Assassins: The KGB's Poison Factory 10 Years On, Frontline Books, Yorkshire (2019)

Woolsey, R. James, and Pacepa , Ion Mihai, Operation Dragon, Encounter Books, New York, (2021)

[1] Shenkman, C., Franklin, S.B., Nojeim B., and Shakur D., (2021) Legal Loopholes and Data Brokers How Law Enforcement and Intelligence Agencies are Buying Your Data from Brokers, Center for Democracy & Technology.

[2] https://the-handmaids-tale.fandom.com/wiki/The_Wall

[3] Shenkman, C., Franklin, S.B., Nojeim, G., and Thakur, D., (2021) *Legal Loopholes and Data for Dollars: How Law Enforcement and Intelligence Agencies are Buying Your Data from Brokers*, Center for Democracy & Technology.

[4] https://www.skillsplatform.org/blog/6-stages-of-grooming-adults-and-teens-spotting-the-red-flags/

[5] *AG Sues Boston for Records About Fired Police Commissioner* (Last Accessed February 19, 2022) https://www.wbur.org/news/2021/08/12/attorney-general-boston-police-public-records-lawsuit (Article dated August 12, 2021)

[6] **Damaged goods** refer to the idea that a person is less than perfect psychologically due to a traumatic experience. https://en.wikipedia.org/wiki/Damaged_goods

[7] *https://montrealgazette.com/news/local-news/former-montreal-police-whistleblowers-say-they-were-silenced*

[8] https://en.wikipedia.org/wiki/Hitler_Youth

[10] *Ed Krayewski, NSA Surveillance Operations Envy of Former Stasi Commander, Reason Magazine, June 28, 2013, https://reason.com/2013/06/28/nsas-surveillance-operations-the-envy-of/*

[11]

https://en.wikipedia.org/wiki/Law_for_the_Prevention_of_Hereditarily_Diseased_Offspring

[12]

https://en.wikipedia.org/wiki/German_Society_for_Racial_Hygiene

[13] The wording of the *Aktion T4* edict in English:

> "Reich Leader Bouhler and Dr. Brandt are entrusted with the responsibility of extending the authority of physicians, to be designated by name, so that patients who, after a most critical diagnosis, on the basis of human judgment [*menschlichem Ermessen*], are considered incurable, can be granted mercy death [*Gnadentod*]. -- A. Hitler"

[14]

http://www.holocaustresearchproject.org/euthan/14f13.html

[15] https://www.britannica.com/event/T4-Program

16
https://en.wikipedia.org/wiki/Aktion_T4#Gassing, see also Lifton on page 86.

[17] Richard Emery and Ilann Margalit Maazel, *Why Civil Right Lawsuits Do Not Deter Police Misconduct: The Conundrum of Indemnification and A Proposed Solution*, 28 Fordham Urb L.J. 587 (2000)

[18] Elizabeth Koh, *The Globe Files Suit Against the Boston Police for Keeping Records of Misconduct Secret*, April 30, 2021. https://www.bostonglobe.com/2021/04/30/metro/globe-files-suit-against-boston-police-keeping-officer-misconduct-records-secret/

[19] Richard Emery and Ilann Margalit Maazel, *Why Civil Right Lawsuits Do Not Deter Police Misconduct: The Conundrum of Indemnification and A Proposed Solution*, 28 Fordham Urb L.J. 587 (2000)

[20] By Unknown author - This file has been extracted from another file, Public Domain, https://commons.wikimedia.org/w/index.php?curid=139965

[21] Peter Schweizer, <u>Profiles in Corruption</u>, Harper Collins (2020), "According to SF election financial disclosures, high-dollar donations to Harris campaign

began to roll in from those connected to the Catholic Church institutional hierarchy" Harris had no ties to the Catholic Church. See also, Campaign Finance Disclosures, www.sfethics.com, "Board members of the Catholic archdiocese-related organization and their family members donated another **$50, 920** to Harris' campaign."

[22] Shannon Lee, *The Picasso Problem, Why We Shouldn't Separate the Art from The Artist's Misogyny*, dated November 22, 2017,
https://www.artspace.com/magazine/interviews_features/art-
politics/the_picasso_problem_why_we_shouldnt_separate_the_art_from_the_artists_misogyny-55120 (Last Accessed February 20, 2022)

[23] A Microwave Gun can be used to scramble the video feed or fry the circuits of a camera or electrical device. See, https://www.counter-intelligence.com/electronic-harassment-and-psychotronic-torture/ (Last accessed: February 8, 2022)

[24]https://www.unwomen.org/en/what-we-do/ending-violence-against-women/faqs/signs-of-abuse (An abusive partner may threaten to turn you in to authorities for illegal activity if you report the abuse, or if you resist.)

[25] Dante Alighieri, The Divine Comedy *Inferno* Canto 8 verse 67.

[26] *Ibid.*, verse 1

[27] Margaret Atwood, <u>The Robber Bride</u>

[28] Nancy J. Perry REPORTER ASSOCIATE Susan Caminiti, A CONSULTING FIRM TOO HOT TO HANDLE? Bain & Co. gets its hands "deep in the trousers of client companies,'" says an executive who knows it well. Maybe too deep, the Guinness scandal suggests. (FORTUNE Magazine) April 27, 1987

[29]
https://www2.psnews.com.au/alerts/psn776APSExtraGraphic.pdf

[30] *Alias* Season 2, Episode 3, Cipher, spoken by Lena Olin, playing mother to Jennifer Garner's character whose alias is Laura. (paraphrasing)

[31] *Bandler, Richard (1997). <u>"NLP Seminars Group – Frequently Asked Questions"</u>. NLP Seminars Group. NLP Seminars Group. Archived from <u>the original</u> on 22 June 2013. Retrieved 8 August 2013.*

[32] Sheridan, Thomas, *Puzzling People, The Labyrinth of the Psychopath*, Velluminous March 1, 2011, see, *A Pawn by Any Other Name: Social Information Processing as a Function of Psychopathic Traits*, "Psychopaths are profoundly aware of a potential target's emotional state – and by extension their

future potential for predatory mind-control after the psychopath is successful in implementing a relationship with the victim." (p. 133) ..the study cited refers to **"Careful selection of victims, targeting the most useful or most easily controlled**." Common factors relevant to selection may include lack of immediate family member contact, smaller social circle or isolation, emotional vulnerabilities, such as empathetic nature capable of exploitation.

33

https://eugenicsarchive.ca/discover/connections/5172ef1 5eed5c60000000023 Eugenics theories tested in concentration camps include Josef Mengele's Twin Studies claiming to measure the medical defenses of twins subjected to weekly injections, a death sentence, whose eyes were later removed. The Nazi experiments served no medical purpose and Mengele escaped to Brazil without ever being prosecuted.

34 By Alex Ross / Dynamite Entertainment - [1], Fair use, https://en.wikipedia.org/w/index.php?curid=54933158

35

Kara Hedash, *Brave New World's Soma Explained* (& Why the Society Relies on The Drug) The society in the focus of Peacock's Brave New World constantly takes a drug called soma. Here's what it does and why the utopia relies on the pills. July 17, 2020, https://screenrant.com/brave-new-world-soma-drug-uses-purpose-explained/ (Last accessed February 20, 2022)

36

https://www.telegram.com/story/news/2021/04/01/tempers-flare-worcester-das-assistant-alleges-due-process-violation-ethics-probe/4822739001/[part of an illegal scheme to excise the statements from the public record?]

37   37

https://www.wbur.org/news/2020/06/24/massachusetts-joseph-early-conflict-of-interest-allegation (Worcester County District Attorney Joseph Early allegedly violated state ethics laws by ordering a prosecutor to alter a police report on the arrest of a judge's daughter, according to a State Ethics Commission's enforcement division.) The report noted above involves a relative of Joseph D. Early.

[38] A better horse will carry a heavier weight, to give him or her a disadvantage when racing against slower horses. The handicapper's goal in assigning handicap weights is to enable all the horses to finish together (in a dead heat). https://en.wikipedia.org/wiki/Handicapping, and   see   also, https://en.wikipedia.org/wiki/Gamblers_Anonymous

[39] *See*, on page 92, https://www.town.westborough.ma.us/sites/g/files/vyhli f5176/f/uploads/budget_detail.pdf

[40] The teacher of the gun class makes crude sexualized statements.

[41] https://journals.lww.com/ajnonline/fulltext/2018/09000/jury_finds_in_favor_of_nurse_who_sued_brigham_and.13.aspx

[42] This comment alone would be sufficient to state a prima facie case of gender discrimination when coupled with the deduction in earnings, especially when viewed in terms of a subsequent female attorney and the more favorable result.

[43] https://en.wikisource.org/wiki/With_God/Indulgenced_Prayers

[44] Chicago and particularly the songs of Peter Cetera repeat every single time I enter a store since 2015, the year of my MELA whistleblower complaint. https://www.dailymail.co.uk/news/article-10393855/Personal-trainer-64-sues-luxury-health-club-refuse-play-old-music.html https://www.nytimes.com/2009/02/10/nyregion/10indulgence.html

[45] https://www.metrowestdailynews.com/news/20191219/partners-healthcare-to-open-new-outpatient-clinic-in-westborough, ("Depending

on how fast the permitting process goes, the clinic is expected to open in 2022, according to Rich Copp, vice president of communications for Partners.)

46 *https://commonwealthmagazine.org/opinion/what-we-need-to-know-about-mass-general-brigham-expansion/*

47

https://www.communityadvocate.com/2021/10/06/westborough-select-board-approves-payment-in-lieu-of-taxes-agreement-with-mass-general-brigham/ **("The first of its kind" pays Westborough money in lieu of taxes.)**

48

https://www.bizjournals.com/boston/news/2021/11/18/ag-healey-submits-blistering-report-on-mass-genera.html

49 https://commonwealthmagazine.org/health-care/healey-says-mass-general-brigham-expansion-will-net-385m-annual-profit/

50

https://www.bostonmagazine.com/health/2018/05/24/brigham-retaliation-nurse-guilty/

51 Sharyl Atkisson, Stonewalled, Harper Collins, New York (2014) on page 7.

52 The Life of Reason, vol.1, 1905. George Santayana.

53

https://www.americanbar.org/groups/litigation/committe

es/privacy-data-security/practice/2019/third-party-doctrine-wake-of-seismic-shift/

[54] *https://www.dw.com/en/russian-opposition-leader-alexei-navalny-sentenced-to-prison/a-56412686*

[55] *www.theguardian.com/commentisfree/2021/aug/19/action-against-corruption-russian-sanctions-oligarchs-alexei-navalny*

[56] (*https://www.names.org/n/jasey/about*) *According to Hebrew: Gift of god". submission from Virginia, U.S. says the name Jasey means "Great warrior peace maker" and is of African Dutch (Afrikaans) origin. This is part of the cover-up, to deflect attention away from a twenty-year pattern of predatory abuse, abuse I asked him about during his representation of me, to which he responded by destroying my client file, and repeatedly torturing me in the privacy of my own home. This is not justice.*

[57] Under **Rule 1.5 (e)** no lawyer may seek to be paid a clearly excessive contingency fee, nor may a lawyer <u>not named</u> in a contingency fee agreement be paid if he was not named in the fee agreement originally (at the time the agreement was signed by the client). Therefore, where attorneys acknowledge that they have no agreement with the client, and further where neither attorney provides any accounting of the work they claim to have performed, neither has any expectation of payment.

[58] Exodus 22:6

[59] Churchill sought a preemptive agreement with Stalin that might stabilize the post-war world and tie the Soviets down in a way that was favorable to British

interests. US Ambassador Averill Harriman, who was supposed to represent Franklin Roosevelt in these meetings, was excluded from this discussion. https://en.wikipedia.org/wiki/Percentages_agreement

[60]The Nazis enacted legislation that made eugenics the law, e.g. *The Law for the Prevention of the Hereditarily Diseased* in exchange, eugenicists were required to tolerate the Nazis antisemitism.

[61] The amount, seemingly arbitrary, bears some resemblance to a $50,950 donation by the Catholic archdiocese to the Harris campaign, according to election donation disclosures.

[62] In popular usage, both in Germany and abroad, *propaganda* was associated with lies. *See,* https://encyclopedia.ushmm.org/content/en/article/ministry-of-propaganda-and-public-enlightenment (Last accessed February 15, 2022)

[63] Neo-Nazis envision the Fourth Reich as featuring Aryan supremacy, anti-Semitism, *Lebensraum*, aggressive militarism and totalitarianism.[6] Upon the establishment of the Fourth Reich, German neo-Nazis propose that Germany should acquire nuclear weapons and use the threat of their use as a form of nuclear blackmail to re-expand to Germany's former boundaries as of 1937.

[64] The Black Hand can be traced to the Kingdom of Naples as early as the 1750s. The English language term specifically refers to the organization established by Italian immigrants in the United States during the 1880s. Some of

the immigrants formed criminal syndicates, living alongside each other and largely victimizing fellow immigrants.
https://en.wikipedia.org/wiki/Black_Hand_%28extortion%29

[65] The medical rally in front of the house employed LOW-T banners on cars, the cars were staged at the Westborough High School parking lot.

[66] Lenore Walker's Cycle of Abuse suggests victims of persecution engage in role-reversal.

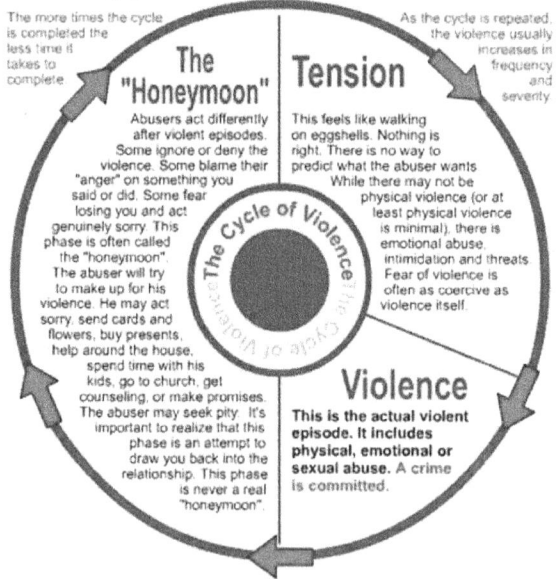

The more times the cycle is completed the less time it takes to complete

As the cycle is repeated, the violence usually increases in frequency and severity.

The "Honeymoon"

Abusers act differently after violent episodes. Some ignore or deny the violence. Some blame their "anger" on something you said or did. Some fear losing you and act genuinely sorry. This phase is often called the "honeymoon". The abuser will try to make up for his violence. He may act sorry, send cards and flowers, buy presents, help around the house, spend time with his kids, go to church, get counseling, or make promises. The abuser may seek pity. It's important to realize that this phase is an attempt to draw you back into the relationship. This phase is never a real "honeymoon".

Tension

This feels like walking on eggshells. Nothing is right. There is no way to predict what the abuser wants. While there may not be physical violence (or at least physical violence is minimal), there is emotional abuse, intimidation and threats. Fear of violence is often as coercive as violence itself.

The Cycle of Violence

Violence

This is the actual violent episode. It includes physical, emotional or sexual abuse. A crime is committed.

[67] *Northeastern University's mascot, Paws is a Siberian Husky, joined by King Husky VIII a bought from dog sled racer Leonhard Seppala.*

[68] Thomas Sheridan, *Puzzling People*, Velluminous March 1, 2011, See on pg 79.

[69] A *Rambaldi[69]* artifact, one of the most famous artworks in antiquity, Pan raping a female goat was discovered in Herculaneum in 1752.

[70] Thomas Sheridan, *Puzzling People*, Velluminous March 1, 2011, See on pgs. 132-133

[71]
https://www.telegram.com/story/news/crime/2020/11/20/ralph-marino-ex-chief-stow-has-child-enticement-case-continued/6361414002/

[72] Michelle the suicide troll's appearance has nothing to do with Irish heritage. This is an attempt to plant emotional landmines..

[73] Thomas Sheridan, Puzzling People, The Labyrinth of the Psychopath Velluminous March 1, 2011.

[74]*https://media2.picsearch.com/is?bWb01InJexbfZu0z6j2E 7r9JLRLjMartxNREQUfQq4o&height=214*

[75] Richard Emery and Ilann Margalit Maazel, *Why Civil Right Lawsuits Do Not Deter Police Misconduct: The Conundrum of Indemnification and A Proposed Solution*, 28 Fordham Urb L.J. 587 (2000)

[76] https://en.wikipedia.org/wiki/Nadia_Santos

[77] *Escheatment,* according to Wikipedia, refers to **Escheat** /ɪsˈtʃiːt/[1][2] is a common law doctrine that transfers the real property of a person who has died without heirs to the crown or state. It serves to ensure that property is not left in "limbo" without recognized ownership. It originally applied to a number of situations where a legal interest in land was destroyed by operation of law, so that the ownership of the land reverted to the immediately superior feudal lord. (*Last accessed February 14, 2022*)

[78] *Indemnification,* according to Wikipedia, may refer to in contract law, **indemnity** is a contractual obligation of one party (*indemnifier*) to compensate the loss incurred to the other party (*indemnity holder*) due to the acts of the indemnitor or any other party. The duty to indemnify is usually, but not always, coextensive with the contractual duty to "hold harmless" or "save harmless". In contrast, a "guarantee" is an obligation of one party assuring the other party that guarantor will perform the promise of the third party if it defaults. In religion, in the context of Unification theology, indemnity is a part of the process by which human beings and the world are restored to God's ideal.[121][122][123][124] The concept of indemnity is explained at the start of the second half of the *Divine Principle,* "Introduction to Restoration":

What, then, is the meaning of restoration through indemnity? When someone has lost his original position or state, he must make some condition to be restored to it. The making of such conditions of restitution is called indemnity. .... God's work to restore people to their true, unfallen state by having them fulfill indemnity conditions is called the providence of restoration through indemnity.[125]

The *Divine Principle* goes on to explain three types of indemnity conditions. Equal conditions of indemnity pay back the full value of what was lost. The biblical verse "life for life, eye for eye, tooth for tooth" (Exod.21:23-24)

[79] **Electronic Harassment.** This required called the plumber to investigate, recalibrate, and eventually, after the fourth time, replace the thermostat which had electronically been manipulated to remain stuck at **66 degrees**, a setting that corresponds to D-Day, June 6.

[80] https://www.congress.gov/bill/114th-congress/senate-bill/766

[81] https://www.peta.org/issues/animal-companion-issues/animal-companion-factsheets/animal-abuse-human-abuse-partners-crime/ (This article also cites related articles of a boy kicking a lamb to death.), and see also, *Assassins*

[82] *Gaslighting.* Leaving this album to be found represents an example of gaslighting. It is letting the owner of the home know that their sense of security is not as it should be, and that someone has gained access to the attic without consent, rearranging it in a way that might cause the owner to question the surroundings and why the

objects have been left there. In the movie *Gaslight*, Secretly, Gregory gains entry into the attic and begins to tamper with the gaslight there, causing the rest of the lamps in the house to become dim. Gregory's diabolical psychopathic behavior becomes very bizarre indeed. Almost immediately he sets out, systematically and methodically, to deliberately drive Paula insane by psychologically manipulating their environment covertly. See, https://narcissisticbehavior.net/the-effects-of-gaslighting-in-narcissistic-victim-syndrome/ (Last accessed: February 21, 2022)

83 Dante Alighieri, The Divine Comedy, Il Purgatorio CANTO 23. Verse 13. Penguin Books London 2013

84 National Academies of Sciences, Engineering and Medicine, 2020, *An Assessment of Illness in US Government Employees and Their Families at Oversees Embassies*, Washington, DC, The National Academies Press.

85   https://vpc.org/revealing-the-impacts-of-gun-violence/female-homicide-victimization-by-males/

86 *See, Tracking Potential Havana Syndrome Attacks on US Soil*

87 Ms. Soleilmavis Lui, mindcontrol - Liu-mindcontrol.pdf

Mindcontrol with Electromagnetic Frequency, (January, 2015) (Last accessed: February 22, 2022)

[88] *Ibid.*

[89] Generally speaking, Democrats get accused of gaslighting more often, however, here we have an example of Republican female-to-female gaslighting. This is more of an observation than an attempt to analyze it. See, https://narcissisticbehavior.net/the-effects-of-gaslighting-in-narcissistic-victim-syndrome/ (Last accessed: February 21, 2022)

www.ingramcontent.com/pod-product-compliance
Lightning Source LLC
Chambersburg PA
CBHW072130280526
45788CB00002B/584